Crochet

FOR BEGINNERS

The Ultimate Guide to Learn Beginner Knots & Patterns From Scratch.
Design Beautiful Creations with Step-By-Step Instructions

Larissa Gordon

COPYRIGHT©2023
BY LARISSA GORDON

Table of Contents

Crochet
FOR BEGINNERS

Book 1

Introduction to Crochet

CHAPTER - 1
Origin of Crochet

The crafts involving a form of a handmade hook or perhaps fingers and fabric to create goods can be traced back as far as the fifteenth century. Many around the globe have claimed their crochet history, but the real origin is still a mystery. However, most historians believe that crochet, as known today, began in the nineteenth Century in England.

8

In Elizabeth Grant's memoirs of Highland Lady published in 1812, the earliest mention of crochet was made about shepherd's knitting. The first crochet patterns were published in the Dutch magazine, Penelope in 1824. Later, in 1829, the term 'crochet' first appeared in the book named 'The ladies knitting and Netting book' which gave instructions about creating a purse using a crochet pattern. Other evidence that crochet was new in the nineteenth century is the 1847 book A Winter's Gift, which includes comprehensive instructions for doing crochet stitches. Before the spelling was standardized in 1848, the first mentions of the craft in Godey's Lady's Book in 1846 and 1847 refer to crochet.

The Danish Shepherd's knitting, now known as slip-stitch, served as the primary inspiration for crochet. The slip-stitch technique was used to make handbags, rugs, and leggings with flat hooks and sharp edges. Later, it was used in the creation of borders, flowers, and accessories.

In the early 1700s, the craft of crochet was believed to be influenced by Tambour embroidery. The French 'tambour' or drum was practiced in china, a technique of creating chain-stitch embroidery using a hook instead of a needle. By the end of the 18th Century, tambour crochet had evolved into a style where the background fabric was not required and the stitching could be done separately. The French gave it the name 'crochet in the air. It was used to make decorative items like lace, hats, and dresses.

HOW DID CROCHET GET ITS NAME?

The term 'crochet' comes from the French word croche which means small hook, or it could be connected to the Norse word krokr, which also means hook. Although the word crochet has French roots it has no evidence that France contributed to the creation of the craft, unlike other countries. The word is used in both French lace-making and Scottish shepherd's knitting.

WHERE DID THE CROCHET HOOK ORIGINATE FROM?

In 1917, Boye Needle co. manufactured the first American Crochet hooks, while the modern crochet hook originated in England in the 19th Century.

The modern crochet hook had evolved from the flat hook used in shepherd's knitting and hooked needle in tambour embroidery, both of which are long-established crafts.

The modern hooks used today are different from the old ones. It is hand-sized, round in cross-section, and has a handle.

In the early 1840s, crochet hooks made of ivory and suitable for yarn appeared primarily in England. Unlike flat hooks, these ivory hooks were unique, similar to modern crochet hooks. Also, these hooks were suggested to beginners for crafts.

ORIGIN OF THE IRISH CROCHET

In the 1840s, Crochet gained popularity in Ireland, as a form of famine relief during the Great Irish Famine. Crocheting was introduced in schools, and Ursuline nuns taught the craft to the Irish men and women as a means to earn money and survive the potato famine instead of just relying entirely on farming.

According to the researchers, in 1846, Mademoiselle Riego de la Branchardiere crafted the lace-like, Irish crochet. Thus, known as the mother of crochet. She wrote the first crochet pattern in her book about clothes and needlework at the age of 18.

The Irish crochet displayed the maker's skill and was carefully created using extremely delicate and lacy stitches and was not intended for everyday wear.

WHEN DID CROCHET BECOME POPULAR IN AMERICA?

The craft of lace reached America when the Irish residents migrated to North America and brought their crochet skills with them. In the late 1940s, after world war I, due to the economic conditions the crochet patterns were significantly simpler and fewer in quantity.

However, during the post-war period, the number of crochet patterns increased and the interest in home crafts grew with creative crochet designs. The locals crocheted colorful bright doilies, afghan blankets, pillows, and other household items. During this time, the famous granny square was also invented, taking crochet to new levels.

The colorful trend continued until the late 1960s and early 1970s, after which interest once more declined.

CROCHET IN THE
Modern Age

After a long period of decline in the 1980s and 1990s, crocheting re- emerged in the 21st century with modern patterns and bright colors. In the fashion world, crochet has experienced a comeback with Cristopher Kane's 2011 collection which extensively featured the most basic crochet,
the granny square.

Similarly recently, Harry style's crochet cardigan from JW Anderson 2020 collection sparked interest in the younger generation.

In addition, craft today has gained popularity as a hobby due to easy access to step-by-step tutorials, free resources, and tools on social media and the internet.

Crochet is also being used as a therapy to help patients reduce stress and anxiety, as well as a means of earning by selling crochet items and patterns over the internet on websites like Instagram, Etsy, and Ravelry.

12

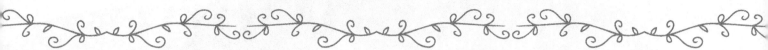

IS CROCHET REALLY DIFFICULT TO LEARN?

Crochet is often perceived as being difficult to learn, but this is not necessarily the case. While it is true that crochet can be a challenging hobby to master, it is also an incredibly rewarding and enjoyable activity. With a bit of patience and practice, anyone can learn how to crochet.

One of the benefits of learning crochet is that it is a relatively simple activity to get started with. All you need is a crochet hook and some yarn, and you can begin practicing basic stitches right away. There are also many resources available to help you learn how to crochet, including online tutorials, instructional videos, and crochet patterns. These resources can provide you with the guidance and support you need to build your skills and confidence.

Another advantage of learning crochet is that it is a very relaxing and therapeutic activity. As you focus on creating your crochet project, you can let go of stress and unwind. Crochet is also a great way to socialize and connect with other people who share your interest in the hobby.

Therefore, don't be intimidated by the idea of learning crochet. With a little bit of practice and the right resources, you can become an accomplished crocheter in no time. So why not give it a try? You may just discover a new hobby that brings you joy and relaxation.

WHAT IS CROCHET?
How to Get Started?

Crochet is derived from the French word 'croche' which means hook. It has been a popular art form used for crafting handmade items from lace trims and doilies to blankets and scarves to an endless range of products. According to Merriam-Webster's definition, Crochet, pronounced as KroSha is 'a needlework consisting of the interlocking of looped stitches formed with a single thread and a hooked needle.'

In other words, Crochet is a type of needlecraft that is created using a hook and yarn stitched into fabric. It is not the name of the fabric itself but rather, the technique of creating the fabric by looping the thread multiple times in different ways around the crochet hook.

Crochet stitches are of different shapes and sizes and a variety of items including garments, accessories, home decor, and more are made using this creative craft.

Although the craft of crochet looks complicated at first it is easy to learn and can be done by anyone with a little practice. It is considered a pleasurable hobby as it is a great way to relieve stress and create beautiful fashion and decor statements for your home or to offer as gifts.

14

WHAT CAN YOU MAKE WITH CROCHET?

Today, crochet has evolved to be a versatile craft used to produce a variety of items. Once you have mastered the skill, you can create so many different crochet projects from wearable to decorative pieces.

Here are 10 easy crochet projects:

Remember, these are just a few examples to get you started. There are endless items to create from crochet, your imagination is the limit. Don't be scared to experiment and be creative!

SWEATER

RIBBED BEANIES

THROW PILLOW

TEA COASTERS

CROCHET PUMPKINS

HAND TOWELS

LAPTOP CASE

TOTE BAG

THE DIFFERENCE BETWEEN KNITTING & CROCHETING

Crochet and Knitting, both are a type of textile art used in making needlework crafts such as blankets and hats. The two are closely related, and seem similar at first but have a few key differences that distinguish the two crafts. The fundamental difference between crochet and knitting is that crochet involves a single hook, while knitting involves two needles.

Here are some key differences between crocheting and knitting:

TYPE	CROCHETING	KNITTING
TOOLS	Done by hand	By Machine or hand
SPEED	Faster	Slower
FABRIC TYPE	Less Stretchy	Stretch Easily
COST	More Costly	Less Costly
EASE OF HOLDING	One Stitch at a time	Multiple Stitches

WHICH IS EASIER? KNITTING OR CROCHETING?

There's no definite answer to which is easier: crocheting or knitting. Some individuals, in the beginning, find holding the two needles a little challenging, and prolonged periods of knitting can result in hand cramps. Likewise, initially, people find crochet to be stiff and less elastic, as they struggle with tension. Thus, there is no simple answer to which is easier and it all comes down to personal preference and which feels more comfortable

Here are some of the reasons why many believe that Crochet is easier than Knitting:

DEXTERITY
Crochet involves one hook instead of two knitting needles, so there are fewer tools to manage at a time making it easier than knitting.

FIXING ERRORS

It is easier to undo a mistake in crochet as you just have to unravel or frog the stitches up to the point where you went wrong and start again. Whereas, stitches in knitting are closely interlocked making it difficult and time-consuming to rip out the stitches.

VARIETY OF SHAPES

It is amazing for making 3-Dimensional shapes without the need for any tools or panels

STRENGTH

Crochet is a series of knots that allows it to make strong and durable materials such as bags, hats, and soft toys.

CONTINUITY

It is also less likely to accidentally unravel because crochet uses one live stitch, this also allows you to start from where you left off.

In the end, it's up to you to decide which craft you want to master first. Learning any new skill requires an equal amount of time and constant practice to develop muscle memory and become proficient.

3 TIPS FOR LEARNING CROCHET

If you are an absolute beginner and decided to crochet, here are THREE great tips to help you in the long run:

 ### PICK AN EASY PROJECT

Choose a pattern that is easy but challenging. You don't want to end up feeling frustrated in the middle of the project.

 ### BEIGIN WITH A SIMPLE PATTERNT

Start with a simple and easy pattern, the more complicated the pattern you learn, the more overwhelmed you will feel. Sharpen your skills on a simple pattern and get a hang of it which will prepare you for the upcoming more complex tasks and patterns.

 ### KEEP PRACTICING

Give your time to learning and practicing the craft. Don't rush through it. Continue learning until you havepracticed enough to perfect the skill.

HOW TO GET STARTED WITH CROCHET?

Crochet is an easy and versatile craft that anybody can learn and practice.
Here are a few ways to start learning how to crochet.

 ### VIDEO TUTORIALS

If you are a visual learner, start by watching crochet step-by- step tutorials on the internet or YouTube. You can even find many tutorials on Udemy from beginner to advanced levels.

 ### PRACTICAL DEMONSTRATION

If you are a hands-on learner, attend a crochet class near you or at craft shops and exhibitions. This is a great way to practice basic stitches under supervision before you try it on your own.

WRITTEN INSTRUCTIONS

 If you prefer to learn through reading, try following written step-by-step instructions in crochet blog articles or a book.

BEGINNER CROCHET SUPPLY

It's equally important to have proper tools when you are first learning to crochet. If you have the right tools and supplies your learning experience will be much smoother and enjoyable.

Here is a list of essential supplies you need to start your crocheting journey:

 ## CROCHET HOOKS

Crochet hooks are the most important and main tool for crocheting. They come in different materials like aluminum, steel, wood, and plastic. Also, are available in thirty different sizes to match the thickness of the yarn. It is recommended to choose a hook that is comfortable to use.

 ## YARN

Yarn is the most fun to experiment with as it comes in various colors, synthetic and natural fibers, and is available in seven different weights. As a rule, thick yarns require thick hooks and thin yarn requires a very small hook. However, it is recommended that beginners start with a light olored, medium-weight yarn and practice with more textured fibers when their skills advance.

 ## YARN NEEDLES

A yarn needle or tapestry needle is a big, blunt tool required to weave in the yarn ends and sew different pieces of crochet together. Metal and plastic yarn needles come in various sizes, and shapes. For starters, it is recommended to use metal needles based on the size of the yarn.

 ## SCISSORS

A pair of scissors is an equally crucial tool for crocheting. They are used to cut threads and trim off edges. There are stock scissors and yarn snips available in the market but any scissor would work as long as it's sharp.

 ## MEASURING TAPE

Measuring tape or scale provides accuracy and perfection in the size of the crochet you are making. You'll need it to measure the length, and width and ensure that a proper gauge is obtained. A flexible tape measure is recommended as it is portable and can be easily wrapped around 3-dimensionalprojects.

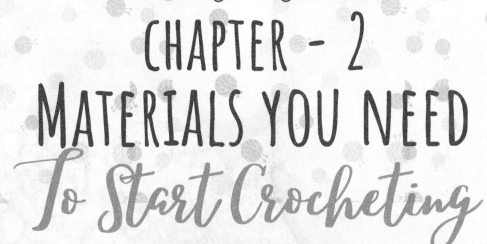

CHAPTER - 2
MATERIALS YOU NEED
To Start Crocheting

Are you curious about what materials you need to start learning crochet? Don't Worry! This Chapter will provide a comprehensive list of the essential crochet supplies and tools that every beginner should have.

Keep reading this chapter for a list of some must-have crochet supplies that you actually need to get started. As a beginner in crochet, it is crucial to have the necessary supplies in order to have a smooth and enjoyable learning experience. Having high-quality tools and craft materials will greatly benefit your journey in learning this craft.

When you are just starting out with crochet, it can be difficult to determine which supplies are necessary and which can be postponed until a later time. In this chapter, I will provide you with a list of the most important crochet supplies and tools that you will need as a beginner crocheter.

♥ The first step is discussing the necessary supplies that are required to begin. These will be referred to as the "need to haves"

♥ Next, I will discuss some additional crochet supplies that can enhance your crochet experience and make it more enjoyable. These are considered "nice to have" items.

♥ I will also provide advice on selecting the appropriate yarn and hooks for your projects to ensure a successful start.

So, whether you are just starting out in crocheting or you are an experienced crocheter looking to expand your tool collection, keep reading for a list of my favorite crochet tools for beginners!

20

CROCHET TOOLS & SUPPLIES

Crocheting requires two essential tools: a crochet hook and yarn. Without these, it will be impossible to create any crochet projects!

To complete your crochet projects, you will need more than just a hook and yarn. Some additional essential items to include in your toolkit are a yarn needle, scissors, stitch markers, and a measuring tape.

The good news is that all of the necessary crochet supplies can easily be found online or at your local craft stores. Now, let's take a closer look at each of these tools and materials.

 CROCHET HOOKS

Before we move on, it's important to discuss the main tool used in crocheting - the crochet hook. Unlike knitting, which utilizes two needles, crocheting is done with a single hook.

There are many choices available when it comes to purchasing a crochet hook. These hooks can be made from different materials, have various shapes, and come in a range of sizes. Each type has its own benefits and drawbacks.

MATERIAL

Crochet hooks are made with a range of materials, such as aluminum, steel, plastic, bamboo, and wood, which can affect the feel of the hook. Metal hooks provide a smooth and quick experience but may be chilly to the touch, while plastic hooks are lightweight and warm, but may have a greater amount of friction on the yarn. There are various materials that crocheting hooks can be made from, such as bamboo, resin, and hand-carved wood. It is a good idea to try out different materials to determine which type of hook you prefer using the most.

SHAPE

Different shapes or styles of crochet hooks are available on the market, such as the Boye brand with a tapered head and throat and a longer shaft, or the Susan Bates brand with an inline-shaped head and throat and a shorter shaft. The Clover Amour brand offers ergonomic hooks with a hybrid shape that falls in between the inline and tapered styles. It is advisable to try out a few different hooks to find your preferred style.

SIZE

The size of the hook needed for your next project will vary based on the pattern and the thickness of the yarn being used. For thin yarns, a thin hook is necessary, while thicker yarns require thicker hooks. If you are unsure of which hook size to use, refer to the yarn label for guidance. After trying out various types of hooks, I have found that metal-tipped hooks with thicker, ergonomic handles are my favorite. The metal tips make it easy for the yarn to glide over them, allowing me to crochet at a faster pace. Additionally, the thicker handles are more comfortable to grip and prevent wrist pain, which can be an issue with thinner metal handles.

THE BEST TYPE OF CROCHET HOOK FOR BEGINNERS

If you are a beginner in crocheting, it is suggested that you start with using aluminum or ergonomic crochet hooks, such as those made by Clover. These types of hooks are designed to be comfortable and easy to use, making them a great choice for those just starting out in the craft.

THE BEST SIZE CROCHET HOOK FOR BEGINNERS

To begin, it is recommended to use a hook that is of medium size, such as a size H (5.0 mm) in combination with yarn that is classified as worsted weight. Another option is to purchase a set that includes various sizes of hooks, specifically those that are commonly used. This way, you will have a range of sizes to choose from as you continue your knitting or crocheting journey.

HOW MANY HOOKS DO YOU NEED?

To begin your crochet project, it is important to select the appropriate hook size for the type of yarn and pattern you have chosen. As you gain more experience and improve your crochet techniques, it may be helpful to have a variety of hook sizes on hand to accommodate different yarn thicknesses and patterns. As you continue to practice and develop your crocheting abilities, having a range of hook sizes will allow you to tackle more challenging projects and achieve the desired results.

BEGINNER'S TIP

There are various labeling systems that are used to indicate the size of crochet hooks in different countries and regions. To make it easier to understand and convert these measurements, it is recommended to use a crochet hook size and comparison chart. This chart will provide detailed information on how to convert one measurement system to another, allowing you to accurately determine the size of your crochet hooks regardless of where you are located. It is important to pay attention to the labeling system being used in order to ensure that you are using the correct Size crochet hook for your project.

  YARN

One of the most delightful aspects of beginning a new crochet project is the process of shopping for yarn. However, when confronted with rows upon rows of yarn at the store, it can be difficult to determine which one is the most suitable for your upcoming project.

When it comes to the art of crochet, there are numerous options for selecting yarn. These options include a wide range of textures, colors, weights, and fiber content. This means that you have the ability to choose yarn that best fits your specific crochet project and desired outcome. The vast array of choices allows for endless creativity and customization in your crocheting endeavors.

TEXTURE

As a beginner, it is advisable to select yarns that are not excessively fluffy, fine, silky, slippery, or bumpy to work with as you practice and improve your crochet skills. Once you have gained more experience and proficiency in crochet, you can then explore and experiment with more textured or delicate fibers.

COLOR

There is a wide range of colors available for yarn, including solid colors, self-striping yarns that feature multiple colors in a single strand, and multicolor yarns that feature a variety of different colors throughout. For those new to knitting or crocheting, it is recommended to start with a lighter colored yarn, as it will be easier to see the individual stitches and track progress. This can be particularly helpful when learning new techniques or patterns.

FIBER CONTENT

There are various types of fibers that yarn can be made of, including synthetic and natural materials like cotton, acrylic, silk, and wool. Among these options, I suggest starting with wool or acrylic-blend yarns because they have a little more resilience and elasticity compared to cotton yarns. This can make them easier to work with and manipulate while learning how to knit or crochet.

WHAT'S THE BEST TYPE OF YARN FOR CROCHET?

As you embark on your first few projects, it is advisable to opt for a medium-weight yarn that has a smooth texture and comes in a lighter shade. Some great options for medium-weight yarns include Lion Brand Wool-Ease and Brava Worsted from WeCrochet. If you desire a more luxurious yarn, Muse Hand-Painted yarn is a good choice. On the other hand,

if you are looking for an inexpensive option, you can consider Red Heart Super Saver yarn.

SCISSORS

If you're a crocheter, a good pair of scissors is an essential part of your toolkit. These scissors will be used to cut yarn and tidy up any stray ends. It's important to have a sharp pair of scissors to make clean cuts and ensure that your projects turn out well. While any pair of sharp scissors will work for crochet, I recommend getting a smaller pair that can easily fit in your crochet bag or project bag. Some options that are particularly cute and functional are yarn snips or stork scissors. Having a compact pair of scissors will make it easy to take your projects on the go and keep everything organized.

CHAPTER - 3
How to Grip?

Let's begin! Make sure you have all the necessary materials and find a well-lit, comfortable area to work in.

Before you start crocheting, it is important to thoroughly read through the instructions. Do not get discouraged if you have difficulty at first, as mastering the craft takes time and practice. Keep at it and you will improve!

Note: This guide uses crochet terminology specific to the United States and includes instructions for crocheting with the right hand.

HOW TO HOLD THE CROCHET HOOK?

The initial action is to familiarize yourself with the proper grip on the crochet hook and yarn. Typically, the crochet hook is held in the hand that is dominant while the yarn is held in the non-dominant hand. It is important to find a grip that feels comfortable for you.

NOTE

As a right-handed individual, the images will depict me using my right hand to hold the hook and my left hand to hold the yarn.

The instructions will be written from the perspective of someone who is right-handed.

However, left-handed individuals can simply reverse the instructions to learn how to crochet with their left hand.

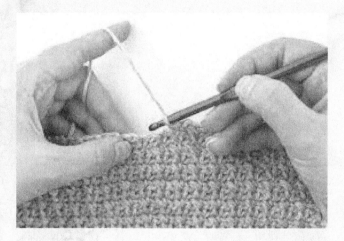

There are two common ways in which people hold a crochet hook: the pencil method and the knife method.

Personally, I find it more comfortable to hold the hook using the knife grip. However, it is important to try both methods and determine which one feels the most comfortable for you.

PENCIL GRIP

To hold the crochet hook, place it between your thumb and index finger as if you were holding a pencil. Use your third finger to provide stability and control by placing it under the hook.

KNIFE GRIP

To hold the crochet hook properly, place your hand over it with your palm facing down. Grasp the hook between your thumb and index finger, and wrap your remaining three fingers around the shaft for added control.

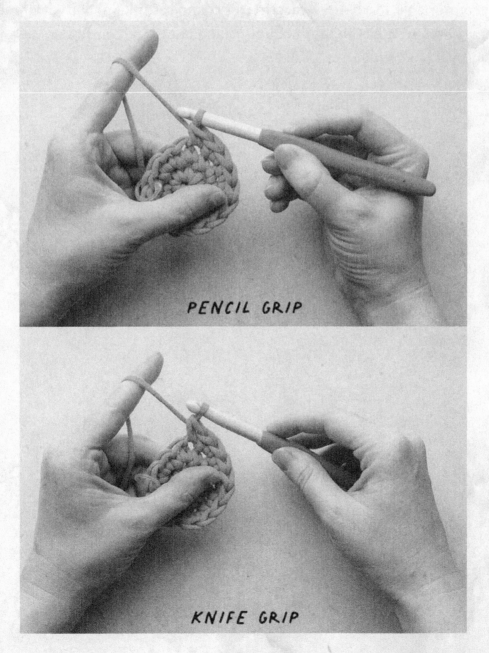

PENCIL GRIP

KNIFE GRIP

27

HOW TO HOLD THE YARN FOR CROCHET?

To hold the yarn, you can place it through the fingers of your non-dominant hand. To do this, pass the yarn over your pinkie finger, under your third and middle fingers, and then over your index finger. To add tension to the yarn, you can also wrap it once around your pinkie finger before passing it under your third and middle fingers and over your index finger.

It may feel uncomfortable to hold the yarn in this manner initially, but with practice, you will discover your preferred method for holding and maintaining tension on the yarn. Don't give up and continue practicing.

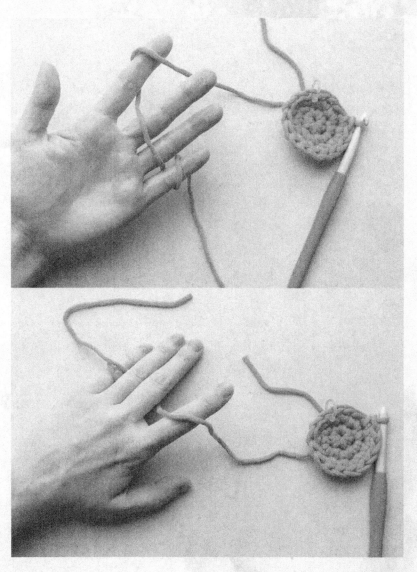

28

CHAPTER - 4
How to Crochet?

Crochet is a versatile craft that involves creating fabric from a hook and yarn. There are various types of stitches in crochet, each with a unique texture and look. In this book, we will cover the basic stitches for beginners including single crochet, double crochet, half double crochet, treble crochet, and slip stitch. These stitches form the foundation for all other crochet patterns and once mastered, will open up a world of creative possibilities.

As you progress through the book, you will learn how to combine these basic stitches to create more intricate patterns and designs.

You will also learn about different types of yarn and hooks, and how to read crochet patterns and charts.

With practice and patience, you will be able to create beautiful, handmade items for yourself and others.

So grab your hook and yarn, and let's get started on your crochet journey!

SLIP KNOT

A slip knot is the starting point for many crochet projects and is used to create a loop on your hook. Here's how to tie a slip knot:

1. Make a loop with your yarn, bringing the tail end over the long end and holding it in place with your fingers.
2. Insert your crochet hook through the loop and grab the long end of the yarn.
3. Pull the long end of the yarn through the loop on your hook, creating a second loop.
4. Tighten the slip knot by pulling on the tail end while holding onto the loop on your hook.
5. The slip knot is now complete and ready to be placed on your hook. You can adjust the tension of the slip knot by pulling on the tail end or the loop on your hook as needed.

It may take a few tries to get the hang of tying a slip knot, but with practice, you will be able to do it quickly and easily. Once you have your slip knot in place, you're ready to begin your crochet project.

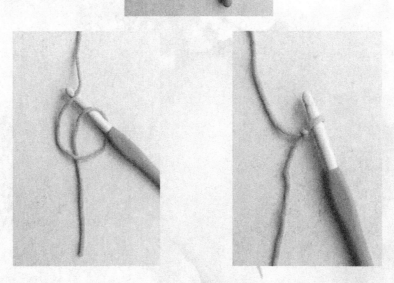

YARN OVER

The yarn-over (abbreviated YO) is a basic crochet technique that is used in all basic crochet stitches. For example, it is used to create a starting chain in the next step and to make single crochet stitches afterwards.

Here's how to yarn over,

1. Bring the working yarn from the back of the hook towards the front, wrapping it around the hook in a clockwise direction.
2. To wrap the yarn over the crochet hook, you can either use your left-hand index finger or pivot the hook under the yarn with your right hand. Both actions achieve the same result.

After you have mastered the YO motion, you can begin incorporating it into the fundamental crochet stitches. Now, let's move on.

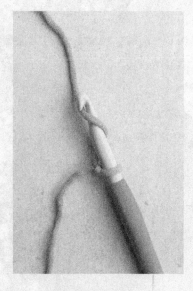

STARTING CHAIN

To continue, the creation of a starting chain is necessary. This is achieved by creating a series of crochet chain stitches, which serves as the base for the rest of the crochet project. To make a starting chain:

1. Use your right hand to hold the hook and your left hand to hold the yarn. Then, insert the hook into the slip knot, if it hasn't already been placed there.
2. With your left hand, grip the end of the slip knot between your thumb and middle finger.
3. Move the yarn currently being used over the hook from the back to the front by pulling it over the hook (also known as a "yarn over").
4. To complete one chain stitch, slightly rotate the hook and catch the yarn in the bowl or mouth of the hook. Then, pull the hook through the loop on the hook.

To create another chain stitch, bring the yarn over the hook and pull it up through the loop. Repeat this action to create the desired number of chain stitches required by the pattern. For example, if the pattern calls for 11 chain stitches, repeat the process 11 times. If you are following along with a swatch, you will need to make 11 chain stitches.

While working, move your left hand fingers along the chain. To have the most control, hold the chain two or three stitches from the hook.

Maintaining consistent tension from chain stitch to chain stitch may require some practice, but with time and repetition, you will develop a natural rhythm. Keep practicing to improve your skills.

Note: When calculating the number of chains you have created, do not include the loop on your hook or the slip knot as part of the total stitch count.

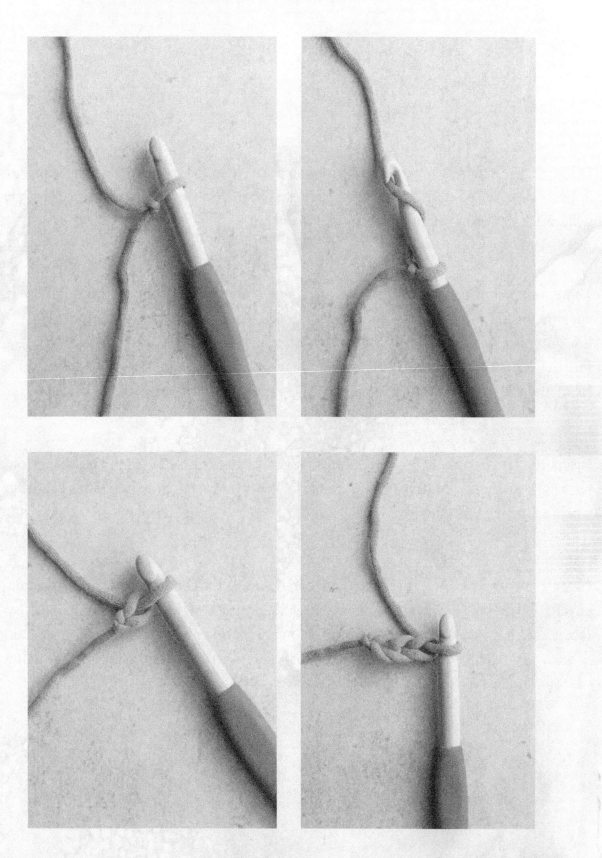

WORKING INTO CHAIN

Examine the chain stitches you have just created more closely. On the front, the chain appears as a series of overlapping V shapes. When you flip the chain over to the back, you will notice that each stitch has a bump or back bar.

To begin crocheting the first row, you will work the stitches into the foundation chain. The specific location of the first stitch may vary depending on the type of stitch being used, and the pattern instructions will specify whether it should be placed in the second, third, or fourth chain from the hook. Once you have completed the first row, you can continue following the pattern instructions to complete the rest of the project.

Insert the crochet hook into the chain stitch, starting from the front and going towards the back. The hook should pass through the center of the V-shaped stitch. This is how you begin working into the starting chain.

If you're new to crochet, the initial row can be quite challenging. It can be difficult to know exactly where to place your hook when working into chain stitches and there isn't much fabric for your other hand to hold onto. However, don't give up! Once you have completed a few rows, you will have a better understanding of where to insert your hook and how to hold the work more securely.

Note: To create a neater edge, some patterns will instruct you to flip the chain and only work the first row of stitches into the back bar. This technique, known as working into the back bar, helps to achieve a cleaner finish.

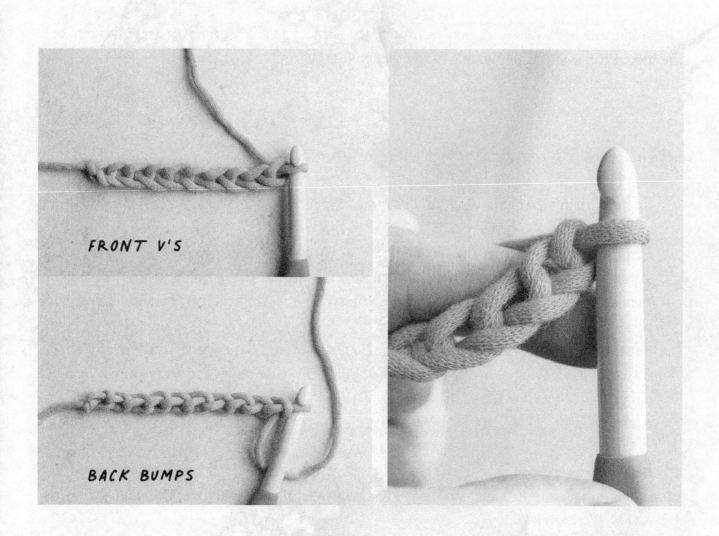

FRONT V'S

BACK BUMPS

SINGLE CROCHET

The single crochet stitch is an easy technique that is perfect for beginners to try. It is one of the most fundamental and widely used crochet stitches and is frequently referred to as SC in crochet instructions.

Let's make the first row of our swatch with single crochet stitches.

1. Begin by using the chain of 11 stitches that we created in the previous section as your starting point.
2. Next, place the hook into the second chain, starting from the hook.
3. To start, place the yarn over the hook and bring it from the back to the front. Then, use the hook to draw the yarn through the chain stitch, creating a loop. You should now have two loops on your hook.
4. To start the single crochet, yarn over the hook. Then, draw the yarn through both loops on the hook, leaving only one loop on the hook. Your first single crochet is now completed.

To create 10 single crochets, repeat these steps by working one single crochet into each of the nine remaining chain stitches. Make sure to avoid twisting the chain while you work.

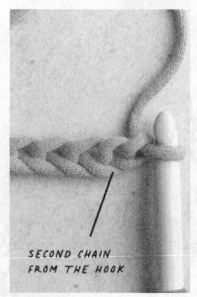

SECOND CHAIN
FROM THE HOOK

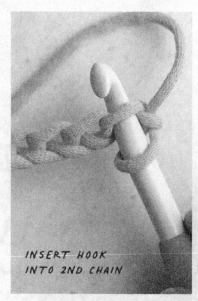

INSERT HOOK
INTO 2ND CHAIN

YARN OVER

PULL UP A LOOP

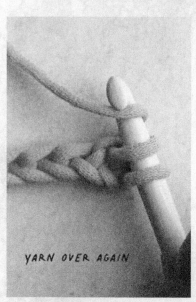

YARN OVER AGAIN

PULL THROUGH
BOTH LOOPS

TURINING CHAIN

At the end of a row, you will flip your work over, create one or more chain stitches (for the turning chain), and then commence the next row of stitches.

Turn the Work

To flip your work, simply rotate it 180 degrees in a clockwise direction. The other side of the work will now be facing you. To ensure I don't lose my place, I maintain the position of my hook in the stitch as I rotate the work.

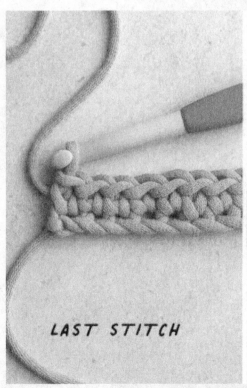

LAST STITCH

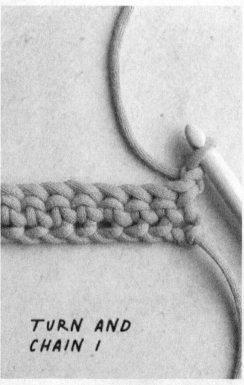

TURN AND CHAIN 1

To begin the next row, you will need to create one or more chain stitches called the turning chain. These stitches will bring the yarn up to the proper height to perform the initial stitch of the following row after you have turned the work.

The height of the stitch in the next row determines the number of chains in the turning chain.

- Single crochet: one chain
- Half-double crochet: two chains
- Double crochet: three chains
- Triple crochet: four chains

Which Comes First: The Turn or the Chain-1?

It doesn't matter whether you turn your work or chain first, you can do either one first.

It is essential to choose a specific method and consistently follow it throughout your work. Additionally, it is recommended to consistently present your work in the same direction, either clockwise or counterclockwise.

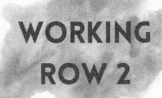

WORKING ROW 2

Let's return to our crochet swatch and begin the second row with single crochet stitches.

These stitches should be worked into the previous row of single crochet stitches, rather than the initial chain.

1. Turn the work and chain 1. (Note that the turning chain used at the beginning of a single crochet row is not considered a stitch.)
2. Insert the hook into the top two loops of the last stitch from the row before, underneath the loops.
3. To create two loops on the hook, start by bringing the yarn from the back to the front. Then, pull the yarn through the stitch, pulling up a loop.
4. To complete a single crochet stitch, yarn over and pull through both loops on the hook. This will leave one loop remaining on the hook.

Begin crocheting from the right side of the row. Create one single crochet stitch in each of the nine remaining stitches. Continue this process until you have completed all stitches.

Double check that you have the correct number of stitches by counting them.

Next, you can begin another row of single crochet stitches.

Continue adding rows until you have reached the desired length. Once you have reached the desired length, cut the yarn and secure it.

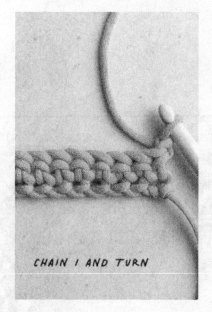

CHAIN 1 AND TURN

INSERT HOOK
INTO 1ST STITCH

YARN OVER

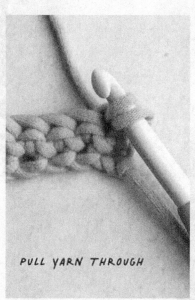

PULL YARN THROUGH

YARN OVER AGAIN

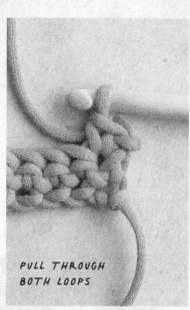

PULL THROUGH
BOTH LOOPS

41

FASTEN OFF

When you have finished the last row of your crochet swatch, you must secure the yarn to prevent the stitches from unraveling. This is called fastening off.

To fasten off:

1. Leave a 6-inch yarn tail and cut the yarn.
2. Pull the yarn tail through the loop on your hook using the hook.
3. Take out the crochet hook from the project, and pull on the end of the yarn to make it tight.

It may be necessary to weave in the yarn tails at this point to ensure they are secure.

To finish off your crochet piece, you'll need to weave in the ends. To do this, take a blunt-tipped yarn needle and thread it with the yarn tail. Next, simply weave the needle back and forth through the crochet fabric.

Congratulations! You have now successfully completed your first crochet swatch.

DOUBLE CROCHET

Double crochet is a basic stitch used in crochet that creates a taller and more open fabric than single crochet. To make a double crochet stitch, follow these steps:

1. Start by making a chain of the desired length.
2. Yarn over (wrap the yarn over the hook from back to front).
3. Insert the hook into the fourth chain from the hook.
4. Yarn over and pull the loop through the chain (you will now have three loops on your hook).
5. Yarn over and pull the loop through the first two loops on the hook.
6. Yarn over and pull the loop through the remaining two loops on the hook.
7. You have now completed one double crochet stitch.
8. Repeat steps 2-7 for each additional double crochet stitch, working into each chain stitch from the row below.

Remember, the height of a double crochet stitch is determined by the number of times you yarn over before inserting the hook into the stitch. Practice makes perfect, so keep working on your double crochet to master it!

HALF DOUBLE CROCHET

Half double crochet (hdc) is a basic stitch used in crochet that creates a taller and less dense fabric than single crochet but shorter than double crochet. To make a half double crochet stitch, follow these steps:

1. Start by making a chain of the desired length.
2. Yarn over (wrap the yarn over the hook from back to front).
3. Insert the hook into the third chain from the hook.
4. Yarn over and pull the loop through the chain (you will now have three loops on your hook).
5. Yarn over and pull the loop through all three loops on the hook.
6. You have now completed one half double crochet stitch.
7. Repeat steps 2-6 for each additional half double crochet stitch, working into each chain stitch from the row below.

It's important to note that the height of the half double crochet stitch is determined by the number of times you yarn over before inserting the hook into the stitch.

Keep practicing to become more comfortable with this stitch. **Good luck!**

44

TREBLE CROCHET

Treble crochet (tr) is a basic stitch used in crochet that creates a taller and more airy fabric than double crochet. To make a treble crochet stitch, follow these steps:

1. Start by making a chain of the desired length.
2. Yarn over twice (wrap the yarn over the hook from back to front twice).
3. Insert the hook into the fifth chain from the hook.
4. Yarn over and pull the loop through the chain (you will now have four loops on your hook).
5. Yarn over and pull the loop through the first two loops on the hook.
6. Yarn over and pull the loop through the next two loops on the hook.
7. Yarn over and pull the loop through the last two loops on the hook.
8. You have now completed one treble crochet stitch.
9. Repeat steps 2-8 for each additional treble crochet stitch, working into each chain stitch from the row below.

Keep in mind, the height of the treble crochet stitch is determined by the number of times you yarn over before inserting the hook into the stitch. Practice makes perfect, so keep working on your treble crochet to master it!

47

SLIP STITCH

A slip stitch (sl st) is a basic stitch used in crochet for a variety of purposes, including finishing edges, connecting pieces, or working in a spiral. Here are the steps to make a slip stitch in crochet:

1. Start with a chain of the desired length.
2. Insert the hook into the next stitch or chain.
3. Yarn over (wrap the yarn over the hook from back to front).
4. Pull the loop through both the stitch and loop on the hook.
5. You have now completed one slip stitch.
6. Repeat steps 2-5 for each additional slip stitch, working into each stitch or chain from the row below.

It's important to note that slip stitches do not add height to your work and are typically used for their ability to create an invisible join or to move the yarn from one place to another without adding bulk.

Practice making slip stitches to become more comfortable with this useful stitch.

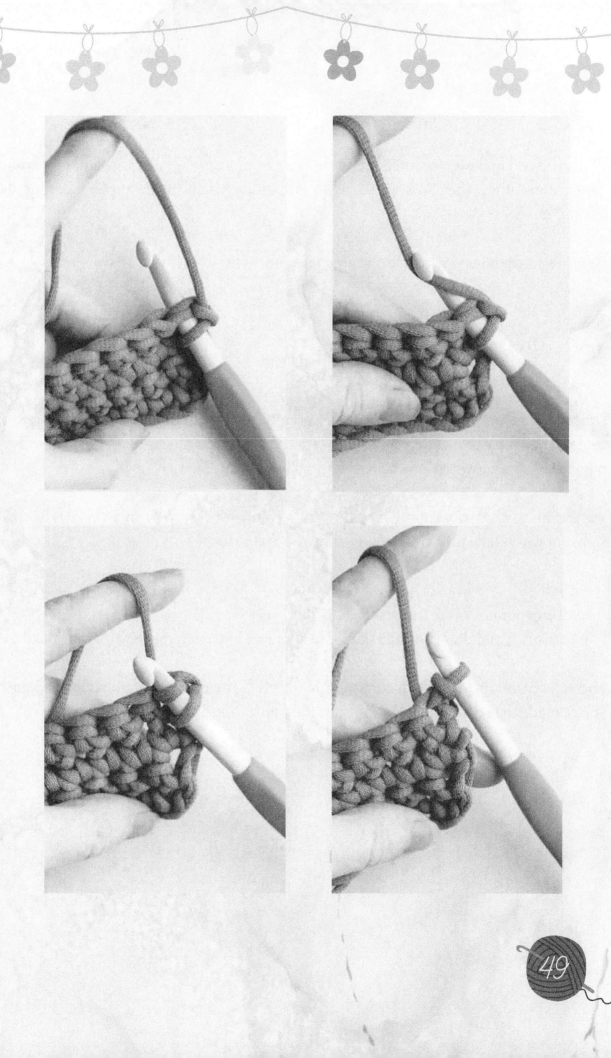

While you can make a crocheted fabric from rows of plain slip stitch, it's not very commonly done. More often, the slip stitch is used as a utility stitch to accomplish another crochet technique.

Here are some other ways to use the crochet slip stitch:

 ## FORMING A CENTER RING

Crochet patterns worked in rounds, like granny squares and top-down hats, start with a center ring. You can make a center ring with the Magic Ring technique, or by joining a small number of chain stitches into a circle with a slip stitch.

For example, your pattern might begin, "Ch 5, join with sl st to form a ring ." The following steps show you how to create a center ring of 4 chain stitches:

1. Chain 5.
2. Insert your hook into the first chain stitch.
3. Yarn over, and draw through the chain stitch and through the loop on the hook.

The slip stitch joins the chain stitches into a circle. The center ring is now complete. After you've made the center ring, you can start the first round of crochet.

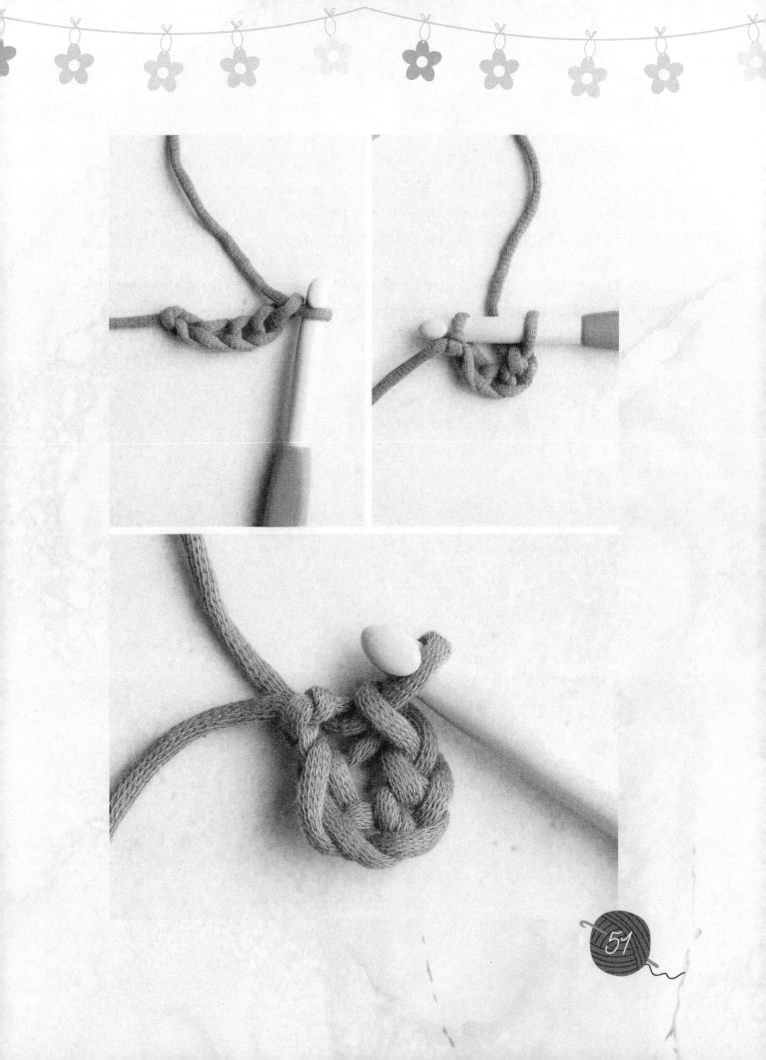

JOINING A ROUND

You can also use a slip stitch to join the end of rounds. The slip stitch will connect the last stitch of the round to the first stitch of that same round.

When you have finished the last stitch of the round, insert your hook into the top of the first stitch of the round. Yarn over and draw through the stitch and the loop on the hook.

Note: This type of slip stitch join is used when working a pattern made in joined rounds, but not in continuous or spiral rounds.

♥ MOVE ACROSS A ROW

You can use slip stitches to move the yarn across a row of stitches without adding much height.

In the picture below, you can see the differing heights of the some of the basic crochet stitches.

The slip stitch is the shortest, followed by the single crochet, the half-double crochet, and the double crochet.

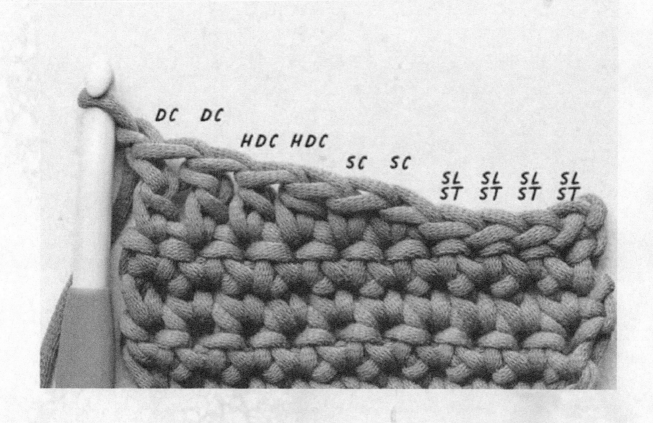

SLIP STITCH SEAM

You can join two or more crochet elements together with a slip stitch seam. For example, you can use slip stitches to join crochet granny squares to create a blanket.

To join two pieces together with a slip stitch seam:

1. Hold the two pieces together with right sides together.
2. Insert the crochet hook into the outer loops (one loop from each of the two pieces.)
3. Yarn over, and pull through the loops on both pieces.
4. Insert the hook through the next two outer loops.
5. Yarn over, and pull through the two outer loops and the loop on the hook.
6. Repeat these steps, crocheting slip stitches across the side of the piece.

SURFACE SLIP STITCH CROCHET

Surface slip stitches are slip stitches worked through the front of your crochet fabric. When finished, they look very similar to an embroidery chain stitch.

You can use surface crochet to decorate the surface of your piece with contrasting colors and stripes.

To work surface slip stitch:

1. Make a slip knot, and hold it at the back of your work.
2. Insert the hook through the fabric, and place the slip knot on the hook. Pull up the loop through to the front side of the work, but keep the knot at the back.
3. Insert the hook into an adjacent stitch (or row, depending on the direction you are traveling)
4. Yarn over and pull through the work and the loop on your hook.

This completes the first surface slip stitch. Repeat these steps until your design is complete.

INCREASE

Increasing in crochet is a technique used to add more stitches to a row, resulting in a wider piece of fabric. Here are the steps to increase in crochet:

1. Work the desired stitch until the last stitch before the increase is complete.
2. Work two stitches into the same stitch or space.
3. Continue with the desired stitch pattern, working one stitch into each of the new stitches created by the increase.
4. Repeat the increase as desired to add additional stitches to the row.

It's important to pay attention to the placement of the increase, as this will affect the overall shape of your work. You can increase at the beginning, end, or middle of a row, or in specific stitches or spaces within a row, depending on the desired pattern. Experiment with different increase techniques to find what works best for you!

SINGLE CROCHET INCREASES

1. Insert the hook under both loops of the indicated stitch.
2. Make a single crochet: Yarn over, and pull up a loop. Yarn over, and pull through two loops.
3. Insert your hook under both loops of the same stitch.
4. Make a second single crochet: Yarn over, and pull up a loop. Yarn over, and pull through two loops.

It really is as simple as that. To increase one stitch in single crochet, simply work two stitches into one stitch.

 ## OTHER CROCHET INCREASES

Single crochet, half double crochet, double crochet, and treble crochet stitches are all increased in the same way: work two stitches into the same stitch.

DECREASE

Decreasing in crochet is a technique used to reduce the number of stitches in a row, resulting in a narrower piece of fabric. Here are the steps to decrease in crochet:

1. Work the desired stitch until two stitches remain before the decrease.
2. Work the next two stitches together, typically by inserting the hook into the first stitch, yarn over, then inserting the hook into the next stitch, yarn over, and pulling the loop through both stitches.
3. Continue with the desired stitch pattern, working one stitch into each of the remaining stitches in the row.
4. Repeat the decrease as desired to reduce the number of stitches in the row.

It's important to pay attention to the placement of the decrease, as this will affect the overall shape of your work. You can decrease at the beginning, end, or middle of a row, or in specific stitches or spaces within a row, depending on the desired pattern.

Experiment with different decrease techniques to find what works best for you!

SINGLE CROCHET DECREASES

You can make a single crochet decrease in a few ways, but the most common method is to crochet two stitches together so that they become one stitch.

Here's how to make a single crochet decrease:

1. Insert hook into the indicated stitch. Yarn over and pull up a loop. (2 loops on the hook.)
2. Insert hook into the next stitch. Yarn over and pull up a loop. (3 loops on the hook.)
3. Yarn over, pull through all 3 loops on the hook.

The single crochet decrease is complete. You should now have only one working loop on your hook.

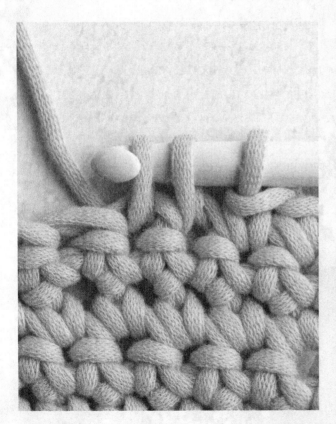

58

WHAT'S ACTUALLY HAPPENING WHEN YOU DECREASE

You may be wondering what's actually happening with all those loops in a single crochet decrease.

Well, the single crochet decrease works by crocheting two stitches together so that they are joined at the top, and become one stitch.

When you make a single crochet decrease, you work the first part of the first single crochet stitch. Then, you move over to the next stitch and work the first part of the second single crochet stitch. Then, you work through all 3 loops on the hook, finishing the single crochet and joining the two stitches together.

OTHER DECREASES

Of course, you can decrease in all types of crochet stitches. You can learn how to decrease in half double crochet (hdc2tog), double crochet (dc2tog), treble crochet (tr2tog). The decreases in other crochet stitches are the same as single crochet decreases.

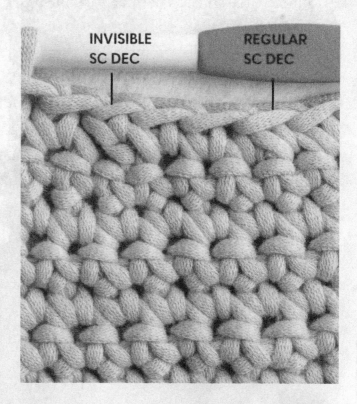

INVISIBLE SC DEC

REGULAR SC DEC

STITCH IN FRONT & BACK OF POST

Stitching in front and back of the post is a technique used in crochet to create a raised texture or design element. Here is how to stitch in front or back of the post:

1. Work the desired stitch until the stitch before the stitch you want to work around the post of.
2. Insert the hook from either the front to back (for a front post stitch) or from the back to front (for a back post stitch) around the post of the stitch, instead of into the top of the stitch.
3. Complete the stitch as normal, working around the post of the stitch.
4. Continue with the desired stitch pattern, working in the front or back post of the stitch as desired.

It's important to note that working around the post of a stitch changes the height and direction of the stitch, creating a raised texture or design element.

Experiment with different post stitch techniques to find what works best for you!

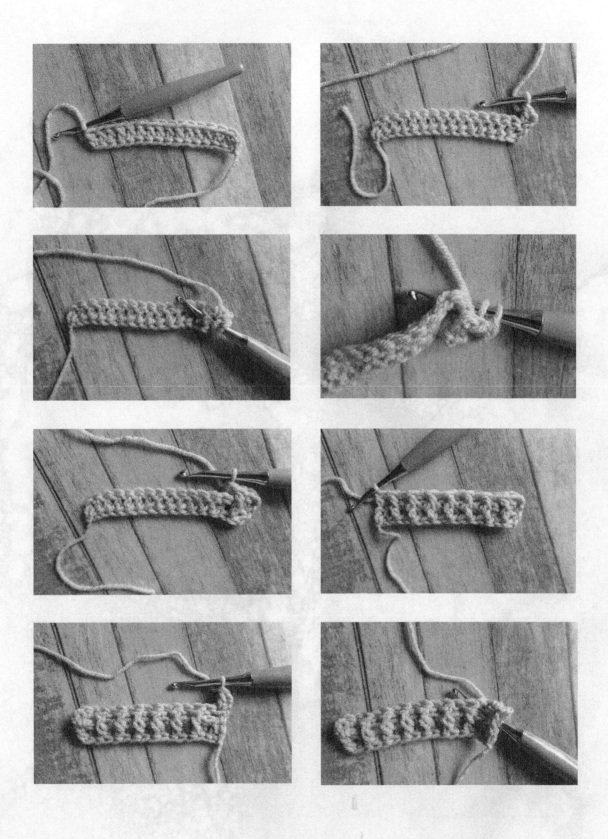

CHAPTER - 5
How to Read Projects?

If you want to start enjoying the creative process of crocheting, it is important to learn how to read crochet instructions. In this guide, I will provide you with the basics of reading crochet patterns, including common language, abbreviations, and important information. Once you have mastered these skills, you can move on to creating your favorite projects with ease.

HOW DO YOU READ A CROCHET PROJEC?

At first, attempting to decipher written crochet patterns may feel like trying to understand a foreign language. However, once you become familiar with the terminology and symbols, you will quickly be able to begin crocheting. To get started, it is essential to familiarize yourself with some basic stitch abbreviations and common crochet terms. To successfully complete your pattern, you must comprehend the necessary requirements including the type of yarn, necessary tools, and gauge.

PART-1: LEARN THE CROCHET LANGUAGE

To be able to comprehend a crochet pattern, it is necessary to familiarize yourself with the basic crochet terminology first. By gaining an understanding of these terms, you will be able to easily use them repeatedly as you continue to crochet.

BASIC STITCH ABBREVIATIONS

These are the abbreviations for the most common crochet stitches that you will come across in crochet patterns. These abbreviations may seem confusing at first, but once you commit them to memory, you will find that they make patterns easier to read and shorter.

- Ch – chain
- Sl st – slip stitch
- Sc – single crochet
- Hdc – half double crochet
- Dc – double crochet
- Tr – treble crochet
- Yo -- Yarn over

Here are some frequently encountered stitch abbreviations in patterns. While it is not necessary to immediately memorize them all, many patterns will remind you of the corresponding stitch names as you go along.

COMMON CROCHET TERMS

In addition to the standard crochet stitch abbreviations, you may come across some commonly used abbreviated terms in crochet patterns. Here are some of the terms you may encounter and their definitions:

- Inc – increase (add one or more stitches)
- Dec – decrease (take away one or more stitches)
- Join – join two stitches together (this is usually done by working a slip stitch)
- Turn – flip your project around so that you can start on a new row of stitches
- Rep – repeat
- Sp – space (refers to crocheting in the space–or spaces–between the stitches)
- St/Sts – stitch or stitches
- Ch-Sp – chain space

PARENTHESES, BRACKETS, & ASTERISKS

Finally, crochet patterns utilize various symbols to indicate how to execute the pattern. Some symbols you may encounter include parentheses, brackets, and asterisks.

How to read crochet pattern parentheses and brackets?

Parentheses ( ) A group of stitches that should be worked together is often referred to as a unit.

Row 4: in next sc work (2 sc, ch 3, 2 sc)

This means that all the stitches within the parentheses are worked into a single crochet stitch. Additionally, parentheses can be used to show how many times a group of stitches should be repeated.

Row 9: Sc in next 3 sc, ch 1, (sc next dc, ch 4, sc in next dc) 4 times, ch 1, sc in next 4 sc

The pattern in parentheses will be repeated 4 times in this row, followed by 1 ch and a sc in the next 4 sc.

Brackets [ ]

Brackets and parentheses are often used in similar ways. They can often be used interchangeably, but brackets are typically used to enclose a group of stitches that need to be repeated.

The following step should be repeated 7 times before proceeding to the next one:

[ch 2, sc in ch 3 sp] 7 times

How to read crochet pattern asterisks?

Finally, asterisks are utilized to indicate a series of repeated stitches or actions. This helps to minimize the need for repeatedly writing out the same steps.

Let's start with a simple example of asterisk use:

Sc in second chain from hook. Sc in each stitch across the row. At the end of the row chain one, turn

Repeat from * to * until the desired width is obtained.

You might often come across this type of example in projects like dishcloths or hot pads, where you have the flexibility to choose the size that works best for you.

Here's another example of asterisk usage:

Round 3: Ch one. Two sc into the next stitch. * One sc. Two sc in the next stitch. Repeat from * to the end. Sl st to join. (18 stitches)

To complete this example, you will repeat the pattern of "one single crochet, followed by two single crochet in the next stitch" until you reach the end of the row.

It is possible to encounter a pattern that employs both a single asterisk (*) and a double asterisk (**) in a single instance, as demonstrated in the following example:

Ch 5, *skip next 2 dc, 1 dc into next dc, [2 dc, ch 3, 2 dc] into next ch 3 sp, **1 dc into next dc; rep from * twice and from * to ** once again, join with sl st into 3rd of ch 5.

If this seems more complex, try taking it step by step. When faced with a challenging instruction like this, try to remain calm and focus on each individual stitch and direction. Proceed slowly and methodically, and you will be able to complete the task successfully.

To recreate the previous example, you will need to crochet from the first single asterisk () to the second single asterisk () twice. After this, you will return to the first single asterisk (*) and crochet to the first double asterisk (**). Finally, you will proceed to the end of the step and join with a slip stitch (sl st).

To make it easier to understand, you can break up each step by adding commas. When you reach a comma, pause and take in the next instruction. It can be overwhelming to try and understand a long line of crochet abbreviations all at once, so breaking it down into smaller pieces makes it more manageable.

PART-2: READING A CROCHET PATTERN STEP BY STEP

Congratulations on learning the basic crochet language! The next step is to familiarize yourself with the standard sections that are typically included in crochet patterns. These sections will provide all the necessary information for completing your project successfully. Don't worry, the rest should be a breeze!

Before starting your project, it's crucial to carefully review the pattern information. This includes using the appropriate yarn and crochet hook size, verifying your gauge, and reading any important pattern notes. Doing so can help prevent hours of frustration and difficulty during the project.

READING CROCHET PATTERNS STEP BY STEP

Here are the standard sections that you will find in most written crochet patterns.

PATTERN TITLE & DESCRIPTION

At the beginning of a crochet pattern, you'll typically find a title and a brief description. Some patterns may also include a difficulty level, which is usually classified as beginner, easy, intermediate, or advanced. This can help you determine if the pattern is appropriate for your current skill level. Keep in mind that even if a pattern is classified as "beginner," it may still require some practice and patience to complete. As you gain experience, you can move on to more challenging patterns.

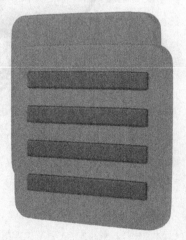

YARNS, TOOLS, & NOTIONS

To ensure that your project turns out as intended, it is important to gather the necessary yarn and supplies. This includes selecting the appropriate hook size and obtaining enough yarn of the correct type. The size of the hook and the weight of the yarn can significantly affect the final size, shape, and texture of your project. Many patterns specify the exact amount of yarn required. For example, a pattern might specify using 75 yards of extra-soft, bulky-weight blanket yarn.

SIZES & MEASUREMENS

Many patterns include information on the expected size of the finished project. For example, a baby blanket pattern might state "Finished size: 30 x 34 inches." To ensure that your crochet project turns out the correct size, it is necessary to use the appropriate size yarn and hook and to check your gauge, which we will discuss in the next section.

GAUGE

To ensure that your project turns out the right size, pay attention to the "gauge" section in the instructions. If size is a factor in the pattern. It is important to crochet a gauge swatch before starting your project to avoid disappointment in the final size of your clothing item.

To follow the gauge instructions for our easy crochet beanie pattern, you will need to know how many stitches and rows you should have per 4 inches. Many patterns will provide this information for you.

Gauge: 12 sts and 7.5 rows per 4".

To achieve the correct gauge for this pattern, you should have 12 stitches and 7.5 rows in a 4-inch square. Please note that some patterns, particularly those worked in the round, may provide gauge instructions differently. For instance, the following is an example of gauge instructions for a bucket hat pattern.

"To test your gauge, crochet the Crown section of the hat pattern (Rounds 1-13) and measure the width of the circle. It should measure 6.5 inches wide.

If your circle is too small, that means your crochet is too tight, and you need to use a slightly larger hook. If your circle is too large, that means your crochet is too loose, and you need to use a slightly smaller hook."

If you notice that your gauge swatch does not match the desired measurements, you may need to adjust the size of your hook by using a slightly larger or smaller one.

STITCH ABBREVIATIONS & TERMS

If you're feeling anxious about the crochet abbreviations and terms we mentioned earlier, don't worry! Most patterns will provide you with a list of the abbreviations you can expect to see, as well as a reminder of what they mean. So, you don't need to worry!

Instructions for uncommon or special stitches will likely be included if they are used in the pattern.

Here's an example of the stitches used in the bucket hat pattern.

- ch = chain
- inc = increase
- sc = single crochet
- sc flo = single crochet through the front loop only
- sl st = slip stitch
- st/sts: stitch/stitches

In most cases, if a pattern includes crochet charts or diagrams, they will be found in the section dedicated to these visual aids.

PATTERN NOTES

You can typically find any specific instructions for your pattern in the pattern notes section. These may include:

- Whether the pattern is written in US vs UK terms
- If a pattern is worked in rows or rounds.
- What is the right side vs. the wrong side
- Whether a pattern is worked in one piece, or will be seamed
- Any other notes the designer thinks may be helpful

MAIN PATTERN INSTRUCTIONS

In the end, you will come across the main pattern instructions. This is where your familiarity with crochet terminology, including stitch abbreviations, will be useful.

Here is an example of some pattern instructions to help you feel confident in your ability to understand and follow a pattern on your own.

For round 3 of this granny square, I will follow these steps. To make it easier to understand, I will provide a translation of each step below.

Round 3:

1. Chain 3. (This counts as 1 dc.)

When you reach the next row, you will notice that chaining three stitches creates the same appearance as one double crochet.

2. Then, into the ch-1 space just below in the previous round, work 2 dc, ch 1. (This makes the first granny cluster of this round.)

To create a granny cluster, you will need to start by working in the space created by a chain stitch in the previous round. Begin by making 2 double crochet stitches, then chain 1. This completes your granny cluster.

3. Into the next ch-3 corner space, work: 3 dc, ch 3, 3 dc, ch 1.

The previous row had a space in the corner made from 3 chain stitches. To continue crocheting, work 3 double crochet stitches in this space, followed by 3 chain stitches. Then, add 3 more double crochet stitches and one more chain stitch.

4. Into the next ch-1 space, work: 3 dc, ch 1.

After that, you will come across a gap created with 1 chain stitch. Within this gap, complete 3 double crochet stitches followed by 1 chain stitch.

Repeat steps 3 and 4 around to the beginning chain.
Finally, join with a sl st to the top of the starting 5. ch-3.

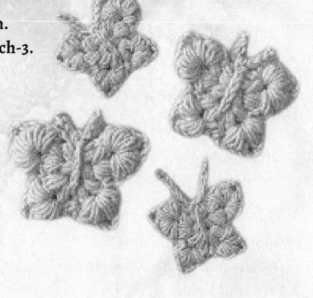

Repeat steps 3 and 4 until you complete
a full circuit around the square. When
you return to the initial 3 chains, use a slip
stitch to secure the yarn. This marks the
completion of the first row of your granny square.

CROCHET TECHNIQUES & TIPS FOR BEGINNERS

Congratulations on deciding to learn how to crochet! It is a rewarding and enjoyable hobby that can produce beautiful and useful items. Here are some tips to help you get started:

• KEEP YOUR STITCHES RELAXED & LOOSE.

It is natural to feel tense when learning something new, and this can cause you to hold your hook too tightly. Try to keep your stitches relaxed and loose to make it easier to insert the hook.

• PRACTICE PRACTICE PRACTICE

Before starting your project, try practicing any new stitches that are used in the pattern. You can also use the gauge swatch, a small sample of crocheted fabric, to practice your technique and ensure that your project will be the correct size.

• EXPERIMENT WITH DIFFERENT TOOLS

If you are having trouble catching the loop on the hook or inserting the hook into the stitches, try using a hook with a deeper bowl or a pointier head.

• TRY DIFFERENT YARNS

Smooth, worsted weight yarns that do not tend to split are a good choice for beginners, but you may prefer a different type of yarn. Experiment to find the yarn that you like best.

• PAY ATTENTION TO GAUGE

Gauge refers to the number of stitches and rows that should fit within a certain number of inches. Make sure to match the gauge specified in the pattern to ensure that your project turns out the correct size.

• DECIDE WHETHER TO FROG

"Frogging" means unraveling your work to correct a mistake. If you notice a mistake a few rows back, you may want to frog it and fix the error, but it is up to you to decide whether the mistake is worth correcting.

• BE KIND TO YOURSELF

Mistakes are a natural part of learning any new skill. Don't be too hard on yourself if you make mistakes, and be proud of yourself for learning something new. With time and practice, you will improve.

CHAPTER - 6
Things to Avoid in Crochet

Crochet is a wonderful and creative hobby, but it can be frustrating if you're just starting out and encounter common mistakes. To help you avoid some of these pitfalls, it's important to pay attention to gauge, keep your tension even, and avoid splitting your yarn. Additionally, it's crucial to follow the pattern instructions carefully and know the basic stitches before attempting more complex designs. By keeping these tips in mind, you can ensure that your crochet projects turn out just the way you want them to.

DO'S AND DON'TS OF CROCHET

Crochet is a fun and rewarding hobby, but to ensure that you have the best experience, it's important to follow some basic do's and don'ts. From using the right size hook to maintaining an even tension, doing things the right way can make all the difference in your projects. On the other hand, there are also common mistakes to avoid, such as crocheting too tightly or using the wrong type of yarn. By familiarizing yourself with these do's and don'ts, you can create beautiful and successful crochet pieces with ease.

DO'S

- Choose the right type of yarn for your project. Some yarns are better for making items like blankets and others are better for making garments.
- Make a gauge swatch to ensure that your finished item will be the correct size.
- Use the correct hook size for your yarn to ensure that your stitch gauge is correct.
- Use a stitch marker to keep track of your place in the pattern.
- Take breaks to avoid hand fatigue and maintain stitch tension.
- Experiment with different stitches and techniques to find what you like best.

DON'TS

- Don't pull your loops too tightly or your work will be stiff and difficult to stitch into later.
- Don't crochet too loosely or your work will look sloppy and be difficult to shape.
- Don't twist your yarn when making a stitch, as this can affect the structure of your work.
- Don't skip stitches or work into the wrong stitch, as this can affect the overall appearance of your project.
- Don't use too many or too few stitches in a row, as this can affect the overall size and shape of your project.

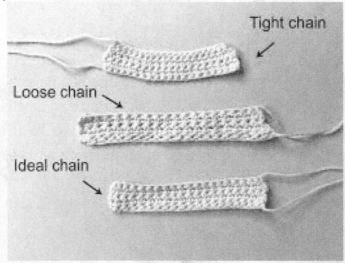

Tight chain

Loose chain

Ideal chain

COMMON CROCHET ERRORS & THEIR TROUBLESHOOTING

Crocheting mistakes are a common occurrence, no matter your skill level. It is helpful to be aware of these common mistakes so that you can avoid them or fix them quickly. Here are 10 common crochet mistakes and some suggestions for how to fix them or prevent them:

ONLY CROCHETING IN FRONT LOOP

This mistake can occur when you are new to crocheting and are not yet comfortable with placing your hook in the proper place for each stitch. To fix this mistake, take some extra time to carefully analyze each row of your work and make sure that you are crocheting under both loops, unless the pattern specifies otherwise.

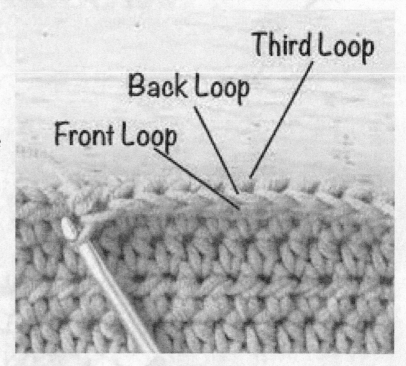

CONFUSING US & UK TERMS

Different countries use different terms for the same crochet stitches. Make sure to check the pattern to see which terms are being used, and familiarize yourself with the terms used in your country.

NOT COUNTING ROWS

Just like you should count your stitches, you should also count your rows. Use a row counter or make a tick mark on a piece of paper after each row to help you keep track.

LOSING COUNT OF YOUR STITCH PATTERN

When working with a repeating stitch pattern, it is easy to lose track of where you are in the pattern. To avoid this mistake, use a stitch marker or place a small piece of contrasting yarn at the beginning of each pattern repeat.

NOT PAYING ATTENTION TO GAUGE

Gauge refers to the number of stitches and rows that should fit within a certain number of inches. Make sure to match the gauge specified in the pattern to ensure that your project turns out the correct size.

TIGHTENING YOUR STITCHES TOO MUCH

If your stitches are too tight, it can be difficult to work with the yarn and your project may be smaller than intended. Relax your stitches to make it easier to work with the yarn.

NOT LEAVING ENOUGH YARN WHEN CHANGING COLORS

When changing colors, make sure to leave a long enough tail of yarn so that you can weave it in later. If you don't leave enough yarn, it will be difficult to neatly hide the ends and your project may look unfinished.

NOT BLOCKING YOUR FINISHED PROJECT

Blocking is a process that involves wetting and shaping your finished project to even out the stitches and give it a polished look. Make sure to block your finished project to give it that professional touch.

Crochet

FOR BEGINNERS

Book 2

CROCHET PROJECTS

Crochet
FOR BEGINNERS

HOUSE
PROJECTS

WALLFLOWER HANGING

These oversized wallflowers are a fabulous way to add a touch of tactile crochet to your living space. While they can be used individually as trivets around your kitchen and dining table, they look absolutely stunning when joined together to create a colour-blocked geometric wall hanging.

TOOLS & MATERIALS

- Size 12mm (US P17) crochet hook

- 500g cones (99.5m/108yd) of Wool And The Gang, Jersey Be Good, one each in shades True Blue, Spearmint Green and Hot Latte

- Yarn needle, wide-eyed blunt

- Scissors

- Sewing needle and strong thread

81

These oversized wallflowers are a fabulous way to add a touch of tactile crochet to your living space. While they can be used individually as trivets around your kitchen and dining table, they look absolutely stunning when joined together to create a colour-blocked geometric wall hanging.

YARN SUBSTITUTION

If you substitute the yarn with another jersey yarn, be sure to use the correct hook, as jersey yarns can vary greatly between manufacturers. This pattern will scale well to suit any hook and yarn size you choose, but remember that using a different size hook and yarn will alter the finished size of your flowers.

TENSION

Individual wallflowers should measure 24.5cm (9/in) in diameter when blocked.

FINISHED SIZE

The wallflower hanging should measure 67cm (26/in) long by 1m (39/in) wide.

When sewing in loose ends of jersey yarn, to easily thread it onto the wide-eyed needle first unroll it. Once flat, fold it in half and thread it through the eye; a few centimetres will be enough it hold it securely.

PATTERN

 ## WALLFLOWERS

Make 9, three each in Spearmint Green, True Blue and Hot Latte.

Foundation ring: using jersey yarn and 12mm hook, ch8, ss to form ring

Round 1: ch3 (counts as first tr), 19tr into ring, ss into 3rd of starting ch3

Round 2: ch2, tr into next st (counts as first tr2tog), ch3, tr2tog over next 2sts rep from to 9 times, ch3, ss into top of first tr2tog

Round 3: ch1, [dc, htr, tr, ch1, tr, htr, dc] into each ch-sp around, ss into first dc, fasten off yarn and weave in loose ends

 ## BLOCKING

First insert your fingers or thumbs into the ch-sp of opposing petals and pull the flower to stretch out the motif; do this with all petals. Then, lay the flower face down and gently steam press on reverse, allowing the steam to penetrate through to the front of the flower. Gently pull the flower into a neat shape, even out the petals and allow to dry fully.

 ## MAKING UP

Joining Flowers: Lay the flowers face down in the colour arrangement shown in the finished photograph. Then, with the sewing needle and strong thread, use a whip stitch to join the petals together at the points marked with a red star on the chart, ensuring that the stitches will not be seen from the right side.

Displaying Hanging: Small panel pins are ideal for displaying the wallflower hanging as they will be hidden amongst the flowers once the display is complete. Five panel pins will be enough for this hanging, one for each flower motif along the top edge. Once you have marked the positions of the panel pins on the wall, hammer each into place leaving 1cm (/in) protruding, which is just enough to hold the hanging without them being seen.

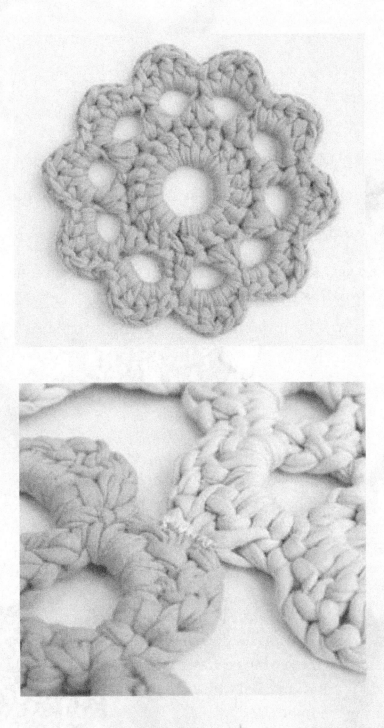

FILET DAISY POTHOLDER

Traditional filet crochet designs are most often seen worked in rows using treble crochet and chain stitches to create a meshlike grid, and by filling the spaces with more treble stitches an array of interesting patterns can be produced. However, the same idea can just as easily be applied to circular motifs, using densely placed treble stitches and increases separated by that familiar open mesh work as can be seen on my Filet Daisy Potholder. It is worked in two layers and the petals of the daisy motif are aligned with joining double crochet stitches to maximize the beautiful filet effect.

TOOLS & MATERIALS

- Size 3mm (US C2 or D3) crochet hook
- 100g balls (280m/306yd) of DMC Petra, size 3, one each in shadesEcru (yarn A), 5722/Orange (yarn B) and 54461/Pale Pink (yarn C)
- Yarn needle
- Scissors

YARN SUBSTITUTION

Any standard 4ply (fingering) weight cotton yarn can easily be substituted for the stated yarn; however, checking your tension carefully beforehand is strongly recommended.

Back Panel

SPECIAL STITCHES

jdc = a double crochet stitch to join the front and back sections of the potholder worked as follows: double crochet into corresponding ch-sp on same round of back section, either immediately before or after tr2tog st of the petal motif

TENSION (GAUGE)

7 rnds in tr sts (12st increase each rnd) = 10cm (4in)

FINISHED SIZE

23cm (9in) diameter (excluding hanging loop)

TIPS & TRICKS

When you come to join the two panels together with jdc stitches, take care to ensure that you are working into the correct row of the back panel. If you are unsure, you could mark the appropriate stitches on each row with a different coloured stitch marker or scrap yarn. Use the symbols shown on the front panel chart as a guide.

86

PATTERN

❤ BACK PANEL

Foundation ring: using yarn A and 3mm hook ch8, ss to form ring

Round 1: ch2 (counts as first htr), 19htr into ring, ss into 2nd of starting ch2

Round 2: ch4 (counts as first htr, ch2), miss one st of prev rnd, htr into next st, ch2 rep from to 9 times, ss into 2nd of starting ch4

Round 3: ss into ch-sp, ch3 (counts as first tr), 2tr into ch-sp, ch1, 3tr into next ch-sp rep from to 9 times, ch1, ss into 3rd of starting ch3

Round 4: ch3, tr into base of ch3 (counts as first 2tr inc), tr, 2tr inc, ch1, miss ch-sp of prev rnd, 2tr inc, tr, 2tr inc rep from to 9 times, ch1, ss into 3rd of starting ch3

Round 5: ch3 (counts as first tr), tr into 4sts, ch1, miss ch-sp of prev rnd, tr into 5sts rep from to 9 times, ch1, ss into 3rd of starting ch3

Round 6: ch3, tr into base of ch3 (counts as first 2tr inc), tr into 3sts, 2tr inc, ch1, miss ch-sp of prev rnd, 2tr inc, 3tr, 2tr inc rep from to 9 times, ch1, ss into 3rd of starting ch3

Round 7: ch3 (counts as first tr), tr into 6sts, ch1, miss ch-sp of prev rnd, tr into 7sts rep from to 9 times, ch1, ss into 3rd of starting ch3

Round 8: ch3, tr into base of ch3 (counts as first 2tr inc), tr into 5sts, 2tr inc, ch1, miss ch-sp of prev rnd, 2tr inc, 5tr, 2tr inc rep from to 9 times, ch1, ss into 3rd of starting ch3

Round 9: ch3 (counts as first tr), tr into 8sts, ch1, miss ch-sp of prev rnd, tr into 9sts rep from to 9 times, ch1, ss into 3rd of starting ch3

Round 10: ch3 (counts as first tr), tr into 8sts, †ch1, tr into ch-sp, ch1†, tr into 9sts rep from to 9 times, rep from † to † once more, ss into 3rd of starting ch3

Round 11: ch2, tr into next st (counts as first tr2tog), †tr into 5sts, tr2tog, ch2, [tr into ch-sp, ch2] twice†, tr2tog rep from to 9 times, rep from † to † once more, ss into top of first tr

Round 12: ch2, tr into next st (counts as first tr2tog), †tr into 3sts, tr2tog, ch2, [tr into ch-sp, ch2] 3 times†, tr2tog rep from to 9 times, rep from † to † once more, ss into top of first tr

Round 13: ch2, tr into next st (counts as first tr2tog), †tr, tr2tog, ch2, [tr into next ch-sp, ch2] 4 times†, tr2tog rep from to 9 times, rep from † to † once more, ss into top of first tr

Round 14: ch2, tr2tog (counts as first tr3tog), †ch2, [tr into next ch-sp, ch2] 5 times†, tr3tog rep from to 9 times, rep from † to † once more, ss into top of first tr2tog, fasten off

front Panel with Edging

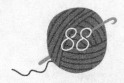

88

♥ FRONT PANEL

This panel is joined to the back panel by sewing the two pieces together at the centre, then joining as you go with joining dc (jdc) sts in rounds 11 to 13.

First: leaving a 30cm (12in) tail of yarn at the beginning, work as given for back panel to the end of rnd 10

Next: lay the back and front panels together, with WS facing, and line up the stitch pattern at the centre. Whip stitch through the centre hole and htr sts of rnd 1; fasten off yarn between the two panels and weave in the loose end

Round 11: line up the petals of the daisy motif and continue with ch3, tr into next st (counts as first tr2tog), †tr into 5sts, tr2tog, jdc into corresponding ch-sp on rnd 11 of back panel, ch1, tr into ch-sp, ch2, tr into next ch-sp, ch1, jdc†, tr2tog rep from to 9 times, rep from † to † once more, ss into top of first tr

Round 12: ch3, tr into next st (counts as first tr2tog), †tr into 3sts, tr2tog, jdc, ch1, [tr into ch-sp, ch2] twice, tr into next ch-sp, ch1, jdc†, tr2tog rep from to 9 times, rep from † to † once more, ss into top of first tr

Round 13: ch3, tr into next st (counts as first tr2tog), †tr into next st, tr2tog, jdc, ch1, [tr into ch-sp, ch2] 3 times, tr into next ch-sp, ch1, jdc †, tr2tog rep from to 9 times, rep from † to † once more, ss into top of first tr

Round 14: work as given for back panel, fasten off

EDGING

All of the sts in rnd 1 of the edging are worked through corresponding sts and ch-sps of both back and front panels together.

Round 1: with front panel facing join yarn B in the top of any tr3tog st (of both back and front panels), ch2, htr into base of ch2, [2htr into ch-sp, htr into next st] 59 times, 2htr into ch-sp, ss into 1st htr (180sts), fasten off

Round 2: join yarn C in 4th htr st of prev rnd, miss 2sts, 8tr scallop into next st, miss 2sts, ss into next st rep from to twice

Hanging loop: dc into 6sts, ch15, working backwards ss into same space as prev ss, working forwards 20dc into ch-sp, ss into same space as 6th dc

Continue round 2: miss 2sts, 8tr scallop into next st, miss 2sts, ss into next st rep from to 27 times (29 scallops + 1 hanging loop), fasten off and weave in loose ends

 # BLOCKING

Using a press cloth, steam press on reverse with a hot iron.

TINY SQUARES PATCHWORK CUSHION

This design was originally inspired by my appreciation of vintage quilt designs, particularly postage stamp quilts made from small squares of fabric. I love how even the simplest design can lend itself to a vast array of interpretations and colour arrangements, although I have always been particularly fond of this classic chequerboard pattern.

TOOLS & MATERIALS

- Size 3.5mm (US E4) crochet hook
- 50g balls (135m/148yd) of Rowan Baby Merino Silk, two in shade 670/Snowdrop (yarn A), three in shade 674/Shell Pink (yarn B), one each in shades 688/Sunshine (yarn C), 692/Leaf (yarn D), 687/Strawberry (yarn E), 694/Frosty (yarn F), 672/Dawn (yarn G) and 696/Lake (yarn H)
- Five 1.5cm (/in) shank buttons
- 40 x 30cm (16 x 12in) cushion
- Yarn needle
- Scissors
- Pins
- Sewing needle and thread to coordinate with yarn B

TENSION (GAUGE)

Each tiny square motif should measure approx. 4cm (1/in) across 21sts
and 12 rows in rows of tr sts = 10cm (4in)

FINISHED SIZE

40 x 30cm (16 x 12in)

TIPS & TRICKS

A great stash-busting project for those precious leftovers that you can't bear to
part with. Each tiny square motif uses approx. 4m (4/yd) of yarn, and if you can
find 40 different colours in your stash, one for each tiny coloured square, you will
be able to crochet a truly unique cushion cover.

PATTERN

 FRONT PANEL

Crochet Tiny Square Motifs:
Make 40 in yarn A; 8 in yarn B; 7 each in yarns C and D; 5 each in yarns E and F; 4 each in yarns G and H.

Foundation ring: using yarn and 3.5mm hook, ch6, ss to form ring

Round 1: ch4 (counts as first tr, ch1), [4tr, ch1] 3 times into ring, 3tr into ring, ss to 3rd of starting ch4

Round 2: ch3 (counts as first tr), †[2tr, ch1, 2tr] into corner ch-sp, miss 1 st of prev rnd†, tr into 3sts rep from to 3 times, rep from † to † once more, tr into 2sts, fasten off invisibly

Join Tiny Square Motifs:
Arrange the tiny square motifs face up in an 8 x 11 grid, matching the arrangement shown in the colour placement diagram to create a chequerboard design.

Using yarn A, join the motifs from the back, working in rows of dc stitches vertically then horizontally. Crochet 1 dc into each corner ch-sp and 1 dc into the top of each side st. When working the horizontal joining rows, simply crochet over the top of the vertical rows when you come to them.

 # BACK PANEL

The back panel is worked in two sections that are crocheted directly onto the front panel along the short ends as follows:

Section 1

Row 1: along first short end of the front panel, with RS facing, join yarn B in the top rightmost corner ch-sp of first tiny square motif, ch2, tr into same space, †tr into 7 sts†, tr2tog over next two corner ch-sps (1st + 2nd motifs) rep from to 7 times, rep from † to † once more, tr into last corner ch-sp (65sts), turn

Row 2: ch2, tr into 7sts, tr2tog, tr into 6sts rep from to 6 times, tr2tog, tr into 8 sts (58sts), turn

Row 3: ch2, tr into 58sts, turn

Rows 4–8: rep row 3

Row 9: with RS facing, join yarn E in rightmost st of prev row, ch1, dc into 58sts, turn

Row 10: ch1, dc into 58sts, turn

Row 11: ch1, dc into 8sts, ch2, miss 1st of prev row, dc into 9sts rep from to 5 times, turn

Row 12: ch1, dc into 9sts, 2dc into ch-sp rep from to 5 times, dc into 8sts, fasten off

Row 13: with RS facing join yarn C in rightmost st of prev row, ch1, dc into 63sts, fasten off

Section 2

Rows 1–3: on the other short end of the front panel work as given for rows 1-3 of section 1

Rows 4–30: rep row 3 of section 1

Row 31: ch1, dc into 58sts, turn

Row 32–34: rep row 31, fasten off

COLOR REPLACEMENTS

- Snowdrop
- Shell Pink
- Sunshine
- Leaf
- Strawberry
- Frosty
- Dawn
- Lake

BLOCKING

The front panel is larger than the back panel, so that when the cushion cover is complete the front panel will wrap around the cushion insert more than in a standard cushion design.

Steam block the front panel to 42 x 32cm (16/x 13in).

Steam block section 1 of the back panel to 28cm (11in) square and section 2 to 10 x 28cm (4 x 11in).

MACKING UP

Join Side Seams

All side seam sts are worked through corresponding sts and ch-sps of both front panel and back panel sections together. First: fold section 2 of the back panel onto the front panel with WS facing, and pin in place along the sides, lining it up with 8 of the tiny square motifs of the front panel

Next: fold section 1 of the back panel and pin in place along the sides, lining it up with the remaining 2 tiny square motifs of the front panel and 1 2 with the contrasting button band overlapping section 2

Next: with RS of cushion facing, join yarn A in corner ch-sp of top rightmost tiny square motif and ch1

Next: work a row of dc sts along the side of the cushion, working into each ch-sp and 8sts of tiny square motifs, joining them to corresponding tr and dc sts of back panel (note that you will work into each tr st twice, the stem and the top of the st) working through three layers at the button band overlap, fasten off

Next: rep for second side seam, fasten off and weave in loose ends

Add Buttons
On row 32 (2nd row of dc sts) of section 2 of the back panel mark 9th, 19th, 29th, 39th and 49th sts with a pin. Sew a button onto each of the marked sts with the sewing needle and thread.

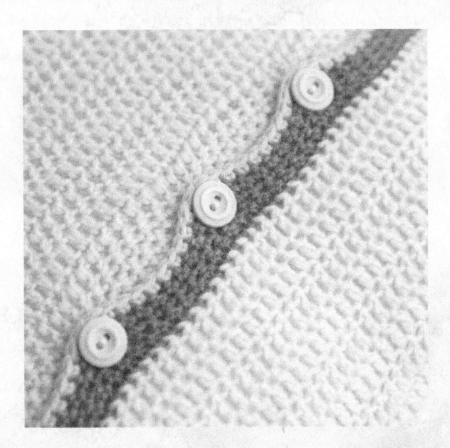

DAISY DOT
LAP BLANKET

We all need a little luxury in our lives, so when selecting yarns for our crochet projects, it pays to choose the best we can, especially when we invest so much of our time on our creations. For this pretty, colourful lap blanket I've chosen a high-quality, super soft, pure alpaca yarn that is surprisingly
budget friendly. It is a joy to crochet with and will make the Daisy Dot Lap Blanket an heirloom piece that you will treasure for years to come.

TOOLS & MATERIALS

- Size 3.5mm (US E4) crochet hook
- 50g balls (167m/183yd) of Drops Alpaca, seven in shade 9020/Light Pearl Grey (yarn A), five in shade 1101/White (yarn B) and one each in shades 2915/Orange (yarn C), 2917/Turquoise (yarn D), 2923/Goldenrod (yarn E), 2921/Pink (yarn F), 3112/Dusty Pink (yarn G), 2916/Dark Lime (yarn H) and 5575/Navy Blue (yarn I)
- Yarn needle
- Scissors

97

YARN SUBSTITUTION

Any standard 4ply (fingering) or lightweight DK (sport) yarn can easily be substituted for the stated yarn; however, checking your tension carefully beforehand is strongly recommended.

TENSION (GAUGE)

7 rnds of circular motif worked in tr sts (12st inc each rnd) = 10cm (4in) Each daisy motif should measure approx. 8.5cm (3/in) diameter

FINISHED SIZE

Approx. 128cm (50/in) long by 94cm (37in) wide

TIPS & TRICKS

If you add the dot motifs as you go, you will find that the work is much easier to handle than if you were to add them at the end once all the daisy motifs have been joined together. So add the first row of dot motifs as soon as the first two rows of daisy motifs have been joined together, then alternate between adding a row of daisy motifs with a row of dot motifs.

PATTERN

♥ DAISY MOTIF

Coloured Centre

Make 165: 24 each in yarns C, D, E and F and 23 each in yarns G, H and I.

Foundation ring: using yarn and 3.5mm hook create an adjustable ring

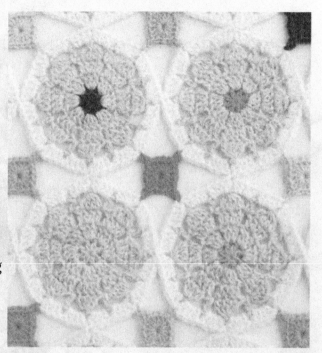

Round 1: ch4 (counts as first tr, ch1), [tr, ch1] 7 times into ring, close ring, ss into 3rd of starting ch4; fasten off

Flower Petals: Make 165 in yarn A.

Round 2: join yarn in any ch-sp, ch4 (counts as first tr, ch1), [3tr, ch1] into 7 ch-sps, 2tr into last ch-sp, ss into 3rd of starting ch4

Round 3: ch4 (counts as first tr, ch1), miss ch-sp of prev rnd, †tr, 2tr inc†, tr, ch1 rep from to 7 times, rep from † to † once more, ss into 3rd of starting ch4

Round 4: ss into ch-sp, ch6 (counts as first tr, ch3), †tr4tog, ch3†, tr into ch-sp, ch3 rep from to 7 times, rep from † to † once more, ss into 3rd of starting ch6, fasten off

Edging/Joining Rounds

Using the colour placement diagram as a guide, arrange the motifs in the correct colour order and work the final round to join the motifs as follows:

99

FIRST ROW:

Motif 1, round 5: join yarn B in any ch-sp before a tr4tog st of prev rnd, ch3 (counts as first tr), 4tr into each ch-sp around, 3tr into last ch-sp (64sts); fasten off invisibly

Motifs 2–11, round 5: join yarn B in any chsp, ch3 (counts as first tr), 4tr into next 12 ch-sps, jn into 17th edging st of first (or prev) motif, 4tr into next 3 ch-sps, 3tr into last ch-sp; fasten off invisibly

SECOND ROW:

Motif 12, round 5: join yarn B in any ch-sp, ch3 (counts as first tr), 4tr into next 8 ch-sps, jn into 2nd edging st of first motif, 4tr into next 7 chsps, 3tr into last ch-sp; fasten off invisibly

Motifs 13–22, round 5: join yarn B in any ch-sp, ch3 (counts as first tr), 4tr into next 8 ch-sps, jn into 2nd edging st of 2nd (or 3rd, 4th, etc.) motif of prev row, 4tr into next 4 ch-sps, jn into 17th edging st of first (or prev) motif in same row, 4tr into next 3 ch-sps, 3tr into last ch-sp; fasten off invisibly

REMAINING ROWS:

Join rows 3 to 15 as given for second row.

 DOT MOTIF

Make 140: 20 each in yarns C, D, E, F, G, H and I.

Each dot motif is crocheted between four daisy motifs, joining them as you go. Using the colour placement diagram as a guide, work each dot motif as follows:

Foundation ring: using yarn and 3.5mm hook ch5, ss to form ring

Round 1: ch3 (counts as first tr), 2tr, ch2, jn into 42nd edging st of top left motif, ch2, ss into top of prev tr st (as in a picot st), 4tr, ch2, jn into 58th edging st of bottom left motif, ch2, ss into top of prev tr st (as in a picot st), 4tr, ch2, jn into 26th edging st of top right motif, ch2, ss into top of prev tr st (as in a picot st), 2tr; fasten off invisibly and weave in loose ends

 BLOCKING

Using a press cloth, steam block on reverse with a hot iron to approx.
128cm (50/in) long by 94cm (37in) wide.

 COLOR REPLACEMENT

- Light pearl gray
- White
- Orange

- Turquoise
- Goldenrod
- pink
- Dusty Pink

- Dark Lime
- Navy Blue

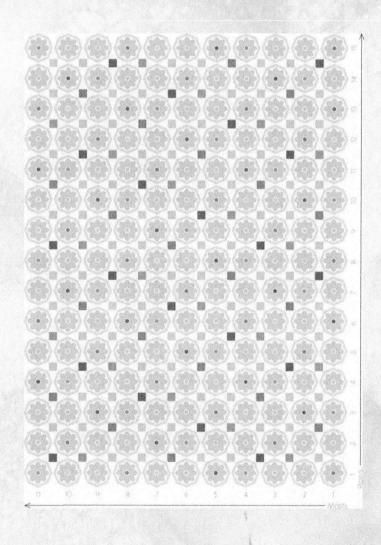

GRANNY CHIC PINWHEEL BLANKET

The humble granny square is a crochet icon that has stood the test of time, providing many crocheters with endless hours of colourful crochet therapy. However, in the spirit of granny chic style, it is always exciting to find new ways to rejuvenate and refresh a classic, so here I've incorporated the granny square into a fabulously pretty pinwheel design. My Granny Chic
Pinwheel Blanket is the perfect blend of retro and modern.

TOOLS & MATERIALS

- Size 4.5mm (US 7) crochet hook
- 100g balls (200m/219yd) of Rowan Pure Wool Worsted, 16 in shade 101/Ivory (yarn A), two each in shades 112/Moonstone (yarn B), 132/Buttercup (yarn C) and 137/Oxygen (yarn D), and one each in shades 113/Pretty Pink (yarn E), 119/Magenta (yarn F), 131/Mustard (yarn G), 134/Seville (yarn H), 135/Papaya (yarn I), 140/Bottle (yarn J), 144/Mallard (yarn K) and 152/Oats (yarn L)
- Stitch holders (small safety pins or scrap yarn)
- Yarn needle
- Scissors

YARN SUBSTITUTION

Any standard DK (light worsted) weight yarn can easily be substituted for the stated yarn; however, checking your tension carefully beforehand is strongly recommended.

TENSION (GAUGE)

Each triangle square motif should measure 28cm (11/in) square 5 rnds of granny square motif worked in tr sts = 10cm (4in)

FINISHED SIZE

Approx. 200cm (78/in) long by 3 4 144cm (56¼in) wide

103

PATTERN

The triangle square motif is crocheted in two halves: the first section in one colour, where the work is turned at the end of each round; the second granny square section in multiple colours, where each round is worked individually in the same direction. It is then crocheted onto the first section and joined at the beginning and end of each round with slip stitches and half treble stitches.

Triangle Square Motif – First Section
Make 35.

Foundation ring: using yarn A and 4.5mm hook, ch6, ss to form ring

Round 1 (RS): ch3 (counts as first tr), 2tr, ch2, 3tr, ch1, turn

Round 2: ch3 (counts as first tr), tr into 4th ch from hook, tr into 2 side sps (between tr sts of prev rnd), [2tr, ch2, 2tr] into corner ch-sp, tr into 2 side sps, f2tr inc into 3rd of ch3 of prev rnd, ch1, turn

Round 3: ch3 (counts as first tr), tr into 4th ch from hook, tr into 5 side sps, [2tr, ch2, 2tr] into corner ch-sp, tr into 5 side sps, f2tr inc into 3rd of ch3 of prev rnd, ch1, turn

Round 4: ch3 (counts as first tr), tr into 4th ch from hook, tr into 8 side sps, [2tr, ch2, 2tr] into corner ch-sp, tr into 8 side sps, f2tr inc into 3rd of ch3 of prev rnd, ch1, turn

Rounds 5–15: rnds 1–3 set the method for the simple single-colour part of the pinwheel, rep these rnds increasing the number of side sts by 3 in each new rnd; at the end of rnd 15 ch2, slip the working loop onto a stitch holder and cut a 15cm (6in) tail of yarn

Triangle Square Motif – Second Section
Make 35.
The colour placement in the second section of each triangle square motif is worked randomly using yarns A–L. However, one ball of yarn A and half a ball of yarn B should be kept aside to work the joining seams and edging.

Round 1: with RS facing, join yarn in ch st at the end of rnd 1 of first section, ch2, [3tr, ch2, 3tr] into foundation ring of first section, htr into base of f2tr inc of rnd 2 of first section, ch1, fasten off

Round 2: with RS facing, join yarn in base of f2tr inc at the end of rnd 3 of first section, ch2, 3tr shell into ch-sp, [3tr, ch2, 3tr] into corner ch-sp, 3tr shell into ch-sp, htr into ch st the end of rnd 2 of first section, ch1, fasten off

Round 3: with RS facing, join yarn in ch st at the end of rnd 3 of first section, ch2, 3tr shell into ch-sp, 3tr shell into side sp, [3tr, ch2, 3tr] into corner ch-sp, 3tr shell into side sp, 3tr shell into ch-sp, htr into base of f2tr inc of rnd 4 of first section, ch1, fasten off

Round 4: with RS facing, join yarn in base of f2tr inc at the end of rnd 5 of first section, ch2, 3tr shell into ch-sp, 3tr shell into 2 side sps, [3tr, ch2, 3tr] into corner ch-sp, 3tr shell into 2 side sps, 3tr shell into ch-sp, htr into ch st the end of rnd 4 of first section, ch1, fasten off

Rounds 5–14: rnds 3 and 4 set the method for adding the granny square part of the pinwheel. Continue in this way, joining a new colour for each new rnd and increasing the number of 3tr shells along each side by 1 in each time

Round 15: join yarn in first ch-sp of prev rnd, ch3 (counts as first tr), 2tr into same sp, 13 x 3tr shell, [3tr, ch2, 3tr] into corner ch-sp, 14 x 3tr shell, ch2, fasten off invisibly to 3rd of starting ch3 of rnd 15 of first section

Finish Triangle Square Motif

Next: using yarn needle, pick up tail of yarn from end of first section and fasten off invisibly to 3rd of starting ch3 of rnd 15 of second section

Blocking Triangle Square Motifs

Steam block each triangle square motif to approx. 28cm (11/in) square.

 ## MAKING UP

Joining Triangle Square Motifs

Arrange the triangle square motifs face up in a 5 x 7 grid, as shown in the photograph, to create a pinwheel design. Using yarn A, join the motifs from the back working in rows of dc stitches horizontally then vertically. Crochet 1 dc into each corner ch-sp (ch-sp and side st where there is a colour change in the corner of the triangle square motif) and 1 dc into the top of each side st. When working the vertical joining rows, simply crochet over the top of the horizontal rows when you come to them.

Edging

Round 1: join yarn A in any corner ch-sp of blanket, ch3 (counts as first tr), tr into top of each st and ch-sp of each triangle square motif along side of blanket, 5tr into corner ch-sp of blanket rep from to to first corner of blanket, 4tr into corner ch-sp, fasten off invisibly

Round 2: join yarn B in first st before any 5tr corner sts of prev rnd, ch1, dc into same sp, [dc, 2dc inc into next 3sts, dc] over next 5 corner sts, dc into each st to next corner rep from to to end, fasten off invisibly

 ## BLOCKING

Using a press cloth, steam block seams and edging so that they lie flat.

Crochet
FOR BEGINNERS

CHRISTMAS PROJECTS

CHRISTMAS TREE POTHOLDER

Christmas time is just around the corner and it's always fun to crochet a few christmas potholders for family and friends. And potholders are easy and quick to crochet! This Christmas potholder is quite simple as it's main stitch in the pattern is Single Crochet. This pattern is designed so that both sides are looking great without the threads of yarn stretching from one side to another or lose ends to weave in. The non-working yarn is carried throughout so no long strings of different yarn are visible on the reverse side.

TOOLS & MATERIALS

- Yarn: 100% Cotton 8 ply/DK/3/Light Worsted (1 skein in white and 1 skein in green)
- Hook: 3.5mm (E-4)
- Yarn needle
- Scissors

STITCHES USED

Single Crochet

TENSION (GAUGE)

20 stitches x 23 rows in pattern = 4"

FINISHED SIZE

17cm x 15cm (6.75" x 6")

PATTERN NOTES

Ch 1 at beginning of row does not count as stitch

Always carry the MC if not in use

PATTERN

Ch 34 with MC (main colour)

Row 1: SC in second chain from hook and across the row (total 33). Ch 1 and turn.

Row 2-4: SC in the first stitch and across the row. Ch 1 and turn.

Row 5: We start to work on the Christmas tree in this row, working from the bottom up.

SC in each of the first 5 stitches, change to CC in the middle of the 5th stitch (watch the video demonstration at the bottom of the page). Work SC in the next 23 Sts and carry the MC along the row crocheting over it. Change back to MC in the middle of the 23d stitch and leave the CC at the back. Continue with MC working SC in the next 5 Sts. Ch 1 and turn.

Row 6: SC in each stitch across with MC. Pick up the CC when you get to the 6th stitch (as shown in the video demonstration) and carry it to the second last St of CC in the previous row. Drop CC yarn to front and complete the row by working SC in each of the remaining stitches. Ch 1 and turn.

Note: for the ease of use I will only put the number of stitches in each colour and row without repeating the instructions on how to do that as they are the same.

Rows 5, 7, 9, 11, 13, 15, 17, 19, 21, 23, 25, 27 are where you change colours. Rows in between are crocheted in main colour (MC) while carrying the contrasting colour (CC) as shown in the video.

Remember to always change colour in the last step of the stitch before.

You can check the number of stitches in each colour in the graph below or continue following the written pattern. (click on the image to enlarge)

109

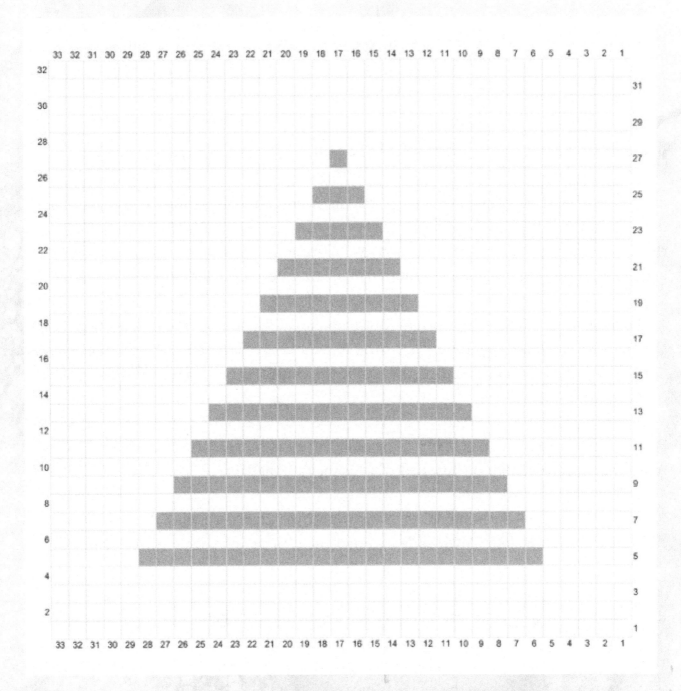

Row 7: 6 SC (mc), 21 SC (cc), 6 SC (mc). Ch 1 and turn.

Row 8: SC across in mc. Ch 1 and turn.

Row 9: 7 SC (mc), 19 SC (cc), 7 SC (mc). Ch 1 and turn.

Row 10: SC across in MC. Ch 1 and turn.

Row 11: 8 SC (mc), 17 SC (cc), 8 SC (mc). Ch 1 and turn.

Row 12: SC across in MC. Ch 1 and turn.

Row 13: 9 SC (mc), 15 SC (cc), 9 SC (mc). Ch 1 and turn.

Row 14: SC across in MC. Ch 1 and turn.

Row 15: 10 SC (mc), 13 SC (cc), 10 SC (mc). Ch 1 and turn.

Row 16: SC across in MC. Ch 1 and turn.

Row 17: 11 SC (mc), 11 SC (cc), 11 SC (mc). Ch 1 and turn.

Row 18: SC across in MC. Ch 1 and turn.

Row 19: 12 SC (mc), 9 SC (cc), 12 SC (mc). Ch 1 and turn.

Row 20: SC across in MC. Ch 1 and turn.

Row 21: 13 SC (mc), 7 SC (cc), 13 SC (mc). Ch 1 and turn.

Row 22: SC across in MC. Ch 1 and turn.

Row 23: 14 SC (mc), 5 SC (cc), 14 SC (mc). Ch 1 and turn.

Row 24: SC across in MC. Ch 1 and turn.

Row 25: 15 SC (mc), 3 SC (cc), 15 SC (mc). Ch 1 and turn.

Row 26: SC across in MC. Ch 1 and turn.

Row 27: 16 SC (mc), 1 SC (cc), 16 SC (mc). Ch 1 and turn.

Row 28-32: SC across in MC. Ch 1 and turn.

Make two of those or make the reverse side plain in any of the colours. Same amount of chains (34), stitches (33) and rows (32).

Stitch them together with the yarn needle or use the slip stitch to crochet them along the sides together and they are done!

Weave in all ends.

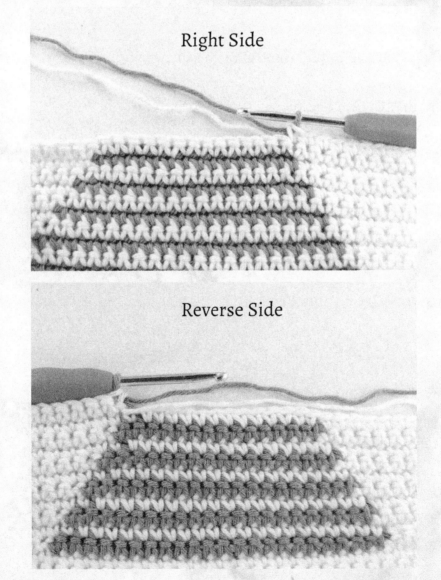

Right Side

Reverse Side

CROCHET SNOWFLAKE COASTER

This crochet snowflake coaster pattern is the perfect winter project for those who love to bring a touch of the holiday season to their home. The intricate snowflake design is made using basic crochet stitches, making it a great project for those who are familiar with the basics of crochet. Not only is it a fun and festive addition to your home decor, but it also serves as a practical piece for keeping your surfaces free from water stains. So, grab your crochet hook and let's get started on creating these beautiful and functional snowflake coasters!

TOOLS & MATERIALS

- Yarn: 100% cotton yarn or a cotton blend, light worsted #3 / 8ply / DK (approx. 15yds/14m in each colour)
- I used Brighton 4 Seasons (50% cotton and 50% Acrylic) in Blue, Snow and Silver.
- Crochet hook 4mm (G)
- Scissors, yarn needle

SKILL LEVEL

intermediate

TENSION (GAUGE)

9 Sts x 10 rows = 2" in single crochet in back loop only

FINISHED SIZE

Length without fringe: 4.5" (11cm) and with fringe: 6.5" (16cm)

Height: 4" (10cm)

SPECIAL STITCHES

Drop-down Double Crochet: work a double crochet in the front loop of stitch 2 rows below. In this pattern, you will work into the same colour front loop 2 rows below as the colour on your hook. In the picture below, the white colour connects two rows below to the white colour again. And the blue colour will connect to blue in future rows.

Drop-down Double Crochet

Drop-down Double Crochet Completed

PATTERN NOTES

- Each row is worked from right to left on the right side (no turning).
- At the end of each row fasten off and cut the yarn, leaving approx. 2-inch tail.
- One colour per row. No need to change colour in the middle of a row.
- Each new row starts with a slip knot and joining new colour to the first stitch in the previous row.
- The first and last stitches are normal single crochet stitches. All other single crochets are worked into the back loop only.
- In the written instructions, when you have a number in front of a stitch, that means you have to work that many of that particular stitch. For example, 5 SC in blo means you have to work one SC in blo in the next 5 stitches.
- You will have yarn ends on each side of your project. The ends will be used to make a fringe.

PATTERN

Ch 22 with A

Row 1: with A, SC in second Ch and across (21). Fasten off and cut the yarn approx. 2 inches away.

Row 2: with A, make a slip knot and attach yarn with a SC to the first St. SC in blo in each St across until the very last St, SC in last St. Fasten off and cut the yarn.

Row 3: with A, make a slip knot and attach yarn with a SC to the first St. SC in blo in each St across until the very last St, SC in last St. Fasten off and cut the yarn.

Row 4: with B, join with SC to first St. SC in blo in each St across until the very last St, SC in last St. Fasten off and cut the yarn.

Row 5: with A, join with SC to first St. 3 dd DC, SC in blo, dd DC, SC in blo, 3 dd DC, SC in blo, 3 dd DC, SC in blo, dd DC, SC in blo, 3 dd DC, SC in last. Fasten off and cut the yarn.

Row 6: with B, join with SC to first St. 5 SC in blo, dd DC, 3 SC in blo, dd DC, 3 SC in blo, dd DC, 5 SC in blo, SC in last. Fasten off and cut the yarn.

Row 7: with A, join with SC to first St. 3 dd DC, 3 SC in blo, dd DC, SC in blo, dd DC, SC in blo, dd DC, SC in blo, dd DC, 3 SC in blo, 3 dd DC, SC in last. Fasten off and cut the yarn.

Row 8: with B, join with SC to first St. 7 SC in blo, dd DC, SC in blo, dd DC, SC in blo, dd DC, 7 SC in blo, SC in last. Fasten off and cut the yarn.

Row 9: with A, join with SC to first St. 5 dd DC, 3 SC in blo, dd DC, SC in blo, dd DC, 3 SC in blo, 5 dd DC, SC in last. Fasten off and cut the yarn.

Row 10: with B, join with SC to first St. SC in blo in each St across until the very last St, SC in last St. Fasten off and cut the yarn.

Row 11: with A, join with SC to first St. 3 dd DC, 5 SC in blo, dd DC, SC in blo, dd DC, 5 SC in blo, 3 dd DC, SC in last. Fasten off and cut the yarn.

Row 12: with B, join with SC to first St. SC in blo in each St across until the very last St, SC in last St. Fasten off and cut the yarn.

Row 13: with A, join with SC to first St. 5 dd DC, 3 SC in blo, dd DC, SC in blo, dd DC, 3 SC in blo, 5 dd DC, SC in last. Fasten off and cut the yarn.

Row 14: with B, join with SC to first St. 7 SC in blo, dd DC, SC in blo, dd DC, SC in blo, dd DC, 7 SC in blo, SC in last. Fasten off and cut the yarn.

Row 15: with A, join with SC to first St. 3 dd DC, 3 SC in blo, dd DC, SC in blo, dd DC, SC in blo, dd DC, SC in blo, dd DC, 3 SC in blo, 3 dd DC, SC in last. Fasten off and cut the yarn.

Row 16: with B, join with SC to first St. 5 SC in blo, dd DC, 3 SC in blo, dd DC, 3 SC in blo, dd DC, 5 SC in blo, SC in last. Fasten off and cut the yarn.

Row 17: with A, join with SC to first St. 3 dd DC, SC in blo, dd DC, SC in blo, 3 dd DC, SC in blo, 3 dd DC, SC in blo, dd DC, SC in blo, 3 dd DC, SC in last. Fasten off and cut the yarn.

Rows 18-19: with A, make a slip knot and attach yarn with a SC to the first St. SC in blo in each St across until the very last St, SC in last St. Fasten off and cut the yarn.

♥ FRINGE

First, we need to add more fringe to our coaster and make it look fuller! Cut both colours into 4-inch pieces. We need 10 pieces of both colours for each side. Take one piece of each colour together, and fold it in half to form a loop. Insert your hook into the first stitches between the yarn tails from underneath and pull the loop halfway through. Take the two tails on each side (see the white-coloured tails in the picture below) and add them to your tassel. Put all the tails through the loop and tighten the knot. After you've done both sides, cut the fringe to 1.5-inch length or as desired. Go through each knot and tighten it a little more, pulling on every strand to make it won't get undone.

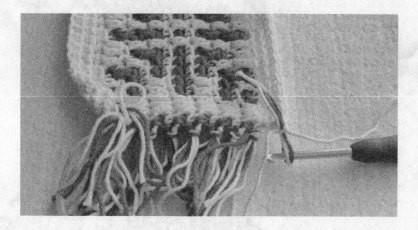

♥ BLOCKING

This mosaic coaster will need blocking. Blocking simply means that you wet the finished project under running water (or use a spray bottle) and then spread it out on a table in the shape you want it to stay. Make sure you have perfectly straight sides and edges with no curling-up corners, as it will keep that shape as it dries.

SNOWMAN GIFT CARD

This snowman gift card crochet pattern is the perfect winter accessory to keep your gift cards organized and secure. Whether you're giving a gift or simply need a place to store your own cards, this cute and quirky snowman design is sure to bring a smile to anyone's face. With its snug fit and easy-to-follow instructions, this pattern is ideal for crocheters of all levels, so grab your hooks and let's get started!

TOOLS & MATERIALS

- Lily® Sugar'n Cream® (70.9 g/2.5 oz; 109 m/120 yds)
- Main Color (MC) (00001 White) 1 ball
- Contrast A (00095 Red) 1 ball
- Small amount of Contrast B (01628 Hot Orange) for Nose.
- Size 4 mm (U.S. G or 6) crochet hook or size needed to obtain gauge.2 black beads for eyes. 3 small red buttons for decoration.

STITCH GLOSSARY

Ch(s) = Chain(s).
Dc = Double crochet.
Hdc = Half double crochet.
Rem = Remaining.
Rnd(s) = Round(s).
Sc = Single crochet.
Sl st = Slip stitch.
Sp(s) = Space(s).
St(s) = Stitch(es).
WS = Wrong side.
Tog = Together.
Yoh = Yarn over hook.

SKILL LEVEL

Easy

TENSION (GAUGE)

15 sc and 16 rows = 4" [10 cm].

FINISHED SIZE

Approx 6" [15 cm] tall.

PATTERN

 BODY

(make 2 pieces alike for Front and Back). **With MC, ch 2.

Round 1: 7 sc in 2nd ch from hook. Join with sl st to first sc. 7 sc.

Round 2: Ch 1. 2 sc in each sc around. Join with sl st to first sc. 14 sc.

Round 3: Ch 1. (1 sc in next sc. 2 sc in next sc) 7 times. Join with sl st to first sc. 21 sc

4th rnd: Ch 1. (1 sc in each of next 2 sc. 2 sc in next sc) 7 times. Join with sl st to first sc. 28 sc.**

5th rnd: Ch 1. (1 sc in each of next 3 sc. 2 sc in next sc) 7 times. Join with sl st to first sc. 35 sc.

6th rnd: Ch 1. (1 sc in each of next 4 sc. 2 sc in next sc) 7 times. Join with sl st to first sc. 42 sc. Fasten off.

JOIN FRONT AND BACK

With WS of Front and Back facing each other, join MC with sl st to any sc. Ch 1. Working through both thicknesses, 1 sc in same sp as sl st. (Miss next sc. 3 dc in next sc. Miss next sc. 1 sc in next sc) 8 times. Fasten off.

 ## HEAD

(make 2). Work from ** to ** as given for Body. Fasten off. Overlap each piece of Head over opening at top of Body and sew in position, leaving opening free as shown in photo.

 ## SCARF

With A, ch 38. 1st row: 1 hdc in 3rd ch from hook and each ch to end of chain. Fasten off.

 ## FRINGE

Cut lengths of A 3" [7.5 cm] long. Take 3 strands tog, fold in half and knot into fringe at each end of Scarf. Trim fringe evenly.

 ## HAT

With A, ch 21. Join with sl st to form a ring, taking care not to twist chain.
1st rnd: Ch 1. 1 sc in each ch around. Join with sl st to first sc.

2nd rnd: Ch 1. 1 sc in each sc around. Join with sl st to first sc.

3rd rnd: Ch 1. (1 sc in each of next 5 sc. Draw up a loop in each of next 2 sc. Yoh and draw through all 3 loops on hook – sc2tog made) 3 times. 18 sts rem.

4th rnd: Ch 1. 1 sc in each st around. Join with sl st to first sc.

5th rnd: Ch 1. (1 sc in each of next 4 sc. Sc2tog) 3 times. 15 sts rem.

6th rnd: Ch 1. 1 sc in each st around. Join with sl st to first sc.

7th rnd: Ch 1. (1 sc in each of next 3 sc. Sc2tog) 3 times. 12 sts rem.

8th rnd: Ch 1. 1 sc in each st around. Join with sl st to first sc.

9th rnd: Ch 1. (1 sc in each of next 2 sc. Sc2tog) 3 times. 9 sts rem.

10th rnd: Ch 1. 1 sc in each st around. Join with sl st to first sc.

11th rnd: Ch 1. (1 sc in next sc. Sc2tog) 3 times. 6 sts rem.

12th rnd: Ch 1. (Sc2tog) 3 times. 3 sts rem. Fasten off. Break yarn. Thread yarn through rem sts pull tightly and fasten securely.

 ## NOSE

With B, ch 3. Sl st in 2nd ch from hook and next ch. Fasten off.

 ## FINISHING OFF

Sew on beads for eyes. Sew Nose in position. Sew 3 buttons to front of Body for decoration. Secure center of Scarf at back of Body. Put on Hat and tie Scarf to keep opening closed.

SNOWFLAKE TABLE RUNNER

Whether you choose a selection of bright colors, soft colors or an elegant shade of white, this table runner will add a happy note to your décor. You'll love using it on a dining table, or adjust the size to fit any table.

TOOLS & MATERIALS

- RED HEART® With Love®: 1 skein each 1803 Blue Hawaii A, 1621 Evergreen B, 1704 Bubblegum C, and 1909 Holly Berry D
- or Holiday colors of choiceSusan Bates®
- Crochet Hook: 5.5mm [US I-9]Yarn needle

SPECIAL STITCH

Picot = ch 4, slip st in last sc made.

TENSION (GAUGE)

1 motif = 6" (15 cm) from point to point, stretched. Gauge is not critical for this project but keep tension tight.

FINISHED SIZE

15" wide x 60" long (38 x 152.5 cm).

SPECIAL TECHNIQUE

Adjustable-ring method = Wrap yarn into a ring, ensuring that the tail falls behind the working yarn. Grip ring and tail firmly between middle finger and thumb. Insert hook through center of ring, yarn over (with working yarn) and draw up a loop. Work stitches of first round in the ring, working over both strands (the tail and the ring). After the first round of stitches is worked, pull gently, but firmly, on tail to tighten ring.

122

NOTES

- Runner is made from 28 snowflake motifs arranged into 3 rows of 9, 10, and 9 motifs each.
- Each motif is worked in joined rounds with right side facing at all times.
- Motifs are sewn to neighboring motifs through center picots in the last rounds. Hold the motifs with wrong sides together as you sew through ch-4 spaces.
- Make and join motifs to neighboring motifs according to Assembly Diagram and instructions.

PATTERN

 RUNNER

Motif (make 28 – 9 with A, 9 with B, 6 with C, and 4 with D)

Make an adjustable ring.

Round 1 (right side): Ch 4 (counts as first dc, ch 1), dc in ring, *(ch 1, dc) in ring; repeat from * 9 times, ch 1; join with slip st in 3rd ch of beginning ch¬—12 dc and 12 ch-1 spaces. Pull gently, but firmly, on tail to tighten ring.

Round 2: Slip st in first ch-1 space, sc in same space, ch 8, sc in next ch-1 space, sc in next dc, *sc in next ch-1 space, ch 8, sc in next ch-1 space, sc in next dc; repeat from * 4 times; join with slip st in first sc—18 sc and 6 ch-8 spaces.

Round 3: Work ([4 sc, picot] 3 times, 4 sc) in first ch-8 space (spoke made), skip next sc, slip st in next 2 sc, *([4 sc, picot] 3 times, 4 sc) in next ch-8 space, skip next sc, slip st in next 2 sc; repeat from * 4 times; join with slip st in first sc—6 spokes. Fasten off.

 FINISHING

With right sides facing, arrange motifs as shown in the assembly diagram. With wrong sides of neighboring spokes held together and matching center picots, sew through ch-4 spaces of center picots to join, matching yarn to one or the other color. Weave in ends. Wet block runner by stretching spokes of each motif evenly, pin in place, and spray with water. Allow to dry thoroughly before handling.

SANTA HAT AND BEARD

Use your crochet skills for a bit of holiday fun. Wearing this Santa hat and beard will make anyone feel like a jolly ol' elf!

TOOLS & MATERIALS

- RED HEART® Super Saver®: 1 skein each 376 Burgundy A and 316 Soft White B.Crochet
- Hook: 6mm [US J-10].
- Yarn needle,
- 4 stitch lock markers.

FINISHED SIZE

Hat measures 22" around.

GAUGE

12 sts = 4"; 14 rows = 4". CHECK YOUR GAUGE. Use any size hook to obtain the gauge.

SPECIAL ABBREVIATIONS

Sc2tog = [draw up a loop in next st] twice, yo and draw through all 3 loops on hook.

Shell = (sc, ch 2, sc) all in next st.

Reverse Sc = Ch 1, insert hook in last st worked and draw through a loop, yo and draw through 2 loops on hook, *insert hook in next st to the right and draw through aloop, yo and draw through 2 loops on hook; repeat from *across.

124

SPECIAL TECHNIQUE

Adjustable ring method = Holding the thread a few inches from the end, wrap around your finger. Do not remove wrap from finger, insert hook into the wrap and draw up a loop of working thread. Chain one to secure the loop and remove ring from finger. Work stitches of first round in the ring. Pull gently, but firmly, on tail to tighten ring.

PATTERN

 ## HAT

With A ch 66; join with a slip st to first ch taking care that ch is not twisted.

Round 1: Ch 1, sc in each ch around; do not join but work in continuous rounds – 66 sc. Place marker in last st and move up each round.

Rounds 2-10: Sc in each sc around.

Round 11: [Sc in next 9 sc, sc2tog] 6 times – 60 sc.

Rounds 12-16: Sc in each sc around.

Round 17: [Sc in next 8 sc, sc2tog] 6 times – 54 sc.

Rounds 18-22: Sc in each sc around.

Round 23: [Sc in next 7 sc, sc2tog] 6 times – 48 sc.

Rounds 24-28: Sc in each sc around.

Round 29: [Sc in next 6 sc, sc2tog] 6 times – 42 sc.

Rounds 30-34: Sc in each sc around.

Round 35: [Sc in next 5 sc, sc2tog] 6 times – 36 sc.

Rounds 36-40: Sc in each sc around.

Round 41: [Sc in next 4 sc, sc2tog] 6 times – 30 sc.

Rounds 42-46: Sc in each sc around.

Round 47: [Sc in next 3 sc, sc2tog] 6 times – 24 sc.

Rounds 48-52: Sc in each sc around.

Round 53: [Sc in next 2 sc, sc2tog] 6 times – 18 sc.

Rounds 54-56: Sc in each sc around; slip st in next sc. Fasten off.

BRIM

Round 1: With wrong side facing, join B in any ch of beginning ch; ch 1, sc in each ch around; do not join but work in continuous rounds as before – 66 sc.

Note: After Round one the brim will flip "up" and you'll be working on the right side.

Rounds 2-9: Sc in back loop of each sc around. At end of Round 9, slip st in back loop of next sc; do NOT fasten off.

Round 10: Work Reverse Sc in each sc to marker. Remove marker.

Note: Rounds 11-18 are worked in a spiral in the unused loops of Rounds 9-2 in descending order.

Rounds 11-18: Work Reverse Sc in each free loop (the remaining front loop) around. Fasten off.

BALL

Round 1: With B, make an adjustable ring, 6 sc in ring; do not join, place marker and move up each round – 6 sc.

Round 2: [2 sc in back loop of next sc] 6 times – 12 sc.

Round 3: Sc in back loop of each sc around.

Round 4: [Sc2tog in back loops] 6 times – 6 sc. Fasten off leaving long tail. Weave yarn through remaining sc, draw up firmly, and fasten securely.

Rounds 5-8: Join B with Reverse sc in last st of Round 4, working in a spiral toward the first st of Round 1, Reverse sc in each st or free loop around. Fasten off leaving long tail. Fold hat point in half to make it narrower; sew ball onto hat tip.

BEARD & MUSTACHE

Starting at Beard with B, ch 33.

Row 1 (Right Side): Working in ridge behind ch only, sc in 2nd ch from hook and in next ch, 2 sc in next ch, [sc in next 8 ch, 2 sc in next ch] 3 times, sc in last 2 ch; turn – 36 sc.

Row 2: Ch 1, working in front loops only, sc in first 2 sc, 2 sc in next sc, [sc in next 9 sc, 2 sc in next sc] 3 times, sc in last 3 sc; turn – 40 sc.

Rows 3 and 5: Ch 1, sc in back loop of each sc across; turn.

Rows 4 and 6: Ch 1, sc in front loop of each sc across; turn.

Row 7: Ch 1, working in front loops only, * shell in next sc; repeat from * across; turn – 40 shells. Now work in free loops of descending rows.

Row 8: Ch 1, working in the free loops of Row 6, shell in each free loop across; turn – 40 shells.

Row 9: Ch 1, working in the free loops of Row 5, [shell in next free loop, skip 1 loop] 19 times, shell in next free loop, sc in last free loop; turn – 20 shells.

Row 10: Repeat Row 9 except work in free loops of Row 4.

Row 11: Repeat Row 9 except work in free loops of Row 3.

Row 12: Repeat Row 9 except work in free loops of Row 2. Mustache

Row 13 (Wrong Side): Ch 1, working in the back loops only of the underside of the foundation ch, [shell, skip next ch] 5 times, ch 15, skip next 13 ch, [shell, skip next ch] 4 times, shell in last ch; turn.

Row 14: Ch 1, working in remaining loops of the same foundation row and in one loop only of the ch-15, [shell, skip 1 st] 16 times, shell in last st – 17 shells. Fasten off.

Row 15: Join yarn to work across the unused loops on the ch-15 only; [shell, skip 1 st] 7 times, shell in last st. Fasten off.

FINISHING

Try the hat on and pin beard to brim to get comfortable fit. With B and yarn needle, whipstitch beard in place to Row 1 of hat brim.

Crochet
FOR BEGINNERS

ACCESSORIES PROJECTS

WAFFLE STITCH CROCHET HAT

The waffle stitch crochet hat is a cozy and stylish accessory for chilly days. The unique texture of the waffle stitch creates a warm and comfortable fabric that is perfect for hats. This pattern is easy to follow, making it a great project for both beginner and experienced crocheters alike.

TOOLS & MATERIALS

- Red Heart® Super Saver™ (7 oz/198 g; 364 yds/333 m)
- Contrast A Aran (0313)
- Contrast B Gray Heather (0400)
- Size U.S. 7 (4.5 mm) crochet hook or size needed to obtain gauge.
- Stitch marker.
- Yarn needle.

GAUGE

13 sc and 14 rows = 4" [10 cm].

MEASUREMENTS

To fit head circumference 18 (20-22)" [45.5 (51-56) cm].

PATTERN

With A, ch 56 (64-72). Join in rnd, taking care to not twist chain.

1st rnd: Ch 2. 1 hdc in each ch around. Join with sl st to first hdc. 56 (64-72) hdc. PM for beg of rnd.

2nd rnd: Ch 2. 1 dcfp around first hdc. *1 dcbp around each of next 3 hdc. 1 dcfp around next hdc. Rep from * to last 3 hdc. 1 dcbp around each of last 3 hdc. Join.

3rd rnd: Ch 2. 1 dcfp around first dcfp. *1 hdc in each of next 3 sts. 1 dcfp around next dcfp. Rep from * to last 3 sts. 1 hdc in each of last 3 sts. Join.

4th rnd: Ch 2. 1 dcfp around first dcfp. *1 dcbp around each of next 3 sts. 1 dcfp around next dcfp. Rep from * to last 3 sts. 1 dcbp around each of last 3 sts. Join.

Rep 3rd and 4th rnds for Waffle Pat until work from beg measures 4" [10 cm], ending on a 4th rnd. Join B. Break A.

With B, rep 3rd and 4th rnds for Waffle Pat until work from beg measures approx 5 (6-61/2)" [12.5 (15-16.5) cm], ending on a 4th rnd.

SHAPE TOP

1st rnd: Ch 2. 1 dcfp around first dcfp. *1 hdc in next st. Hdc2tog. 1 dcfp around next dcfp. Rep from * to last 3 sts. 1 hdc in next st. Hdc2tog. Join. 42 (48-54) sts.

2nd rnd: Ch 2. 1 dcfp around first dcfp. *1 dcbp around each of next 2 sts. 1 dcfp around next dcfp. Rep from * to last 2 sts. 1 dcbp around each of last 2 sts. Join.

3rd rnd: Ch 2. 1 dcfp around first dcfp. *Hdc2tog. 1 dcfp around next dcfp. Rep from * to last 2 sts. Hdc2tog. Join. 28 (32-36) sts.

4th rnd: Ch 2. 1 dcfp around first dcfp. *1 dcbp around next st. 1 dcfp around next dcfp. Rep from * to last st. 1 dcbp around last st. Join.

5th rnd: Ch 2. 1 dcfp around first dcfp. *Skip next st. 1 dcfp around next dcfp. Rep from * to last st. Skip last st. Join. 14 (16-18) sts.

6th rnd: Ch 2. 1 hdc in same sp as sl st and in each st around. Join.

7th rnd: Ch 2. (Hdc2tog) 7 (8-9) times. Fasten off, leaving a long end. Draw end through rem sts. Pull tightly. Fasten securely.

 POMPOM

Wind A around 3 fingers 100 times. Tie tightly in the middle and leave a long end for attaching to Hat. Cut loops at both ends and trim to smooth round shape. Sew securely to top of Hat.

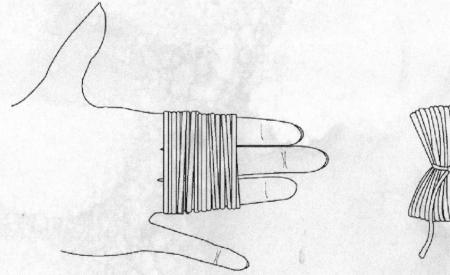

COLORFUL BLOCK CROCHET SCARF

Get ready to add some vibrant hues to your winter wardrobe with this colorful block crochet scarf project! This beginner-friendly pattern uses simple crochet stitches to create a warm and cozy scarf that will brighten up any outfit.

TOOLS & MATERIALS

- Caron® Simply Soft® O'Go™ (5 oz/141 g; 250 yds/228 m)
- Contrast A and B: Harvest Red/Soft Pink (40019) 2 O'Gos
- Contrast C and D: Gold/Orchid (40021) 2 O'Gos
- Size U.S. H/8 (5 mm) crochet hook or size needed to obtain gauge.
- Yarn needle.

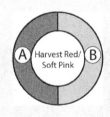
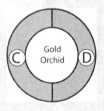

MEASUREMENTS

Approx 10" x 82" [25.5 x 208 cm], excluding fringe.

GAUGE

13 dc and 7 rows = 4" [10 cm].

PATTERN NOTES

• To begin working with the O'Go format, carefully cut plastic tie where the ends of the O'Go meet.

• Pull tie to remove.
For this pattern, colors can be easily separated by gently pulling a part and cutting at the color transition. Each color is ready to use.

• Refer to Materials section for color plan for Contrast A, B, C and D.

• Ch 3 at beg of rows counts as dc.

• To change color, work to last 2 loops on hook and draw new color through last 2 loops, then proceed in new color.

• There is no RS or WS. Scarf is reversible.

PATTERN

 SCARF

Section 1: With A (Color 1), ch 16. Do not break A, cont with B (Color 2) and ch 18.

1st row: With B, 1 dc in 4th ch from hook (counts as 2 dc). 1 dc in each of next 14 ch, joining A. With A, 1 dc in each ch to end of ch. Turn. 32 dc.

2nd row: With A, ch 3. 1 dc in each of next 15 dc, joining B. With B, 1 dc in each ch to end of ch. Turn. 32 dc.

13rd row: With B, ch 3. 1 dc in each of next 15 dc, joining A. With A, 1 dc in each ch to end of ch. Turn. 32 dc.

4th to 9th rows: Rep 2nd and 3rd rows 3 times more, joining D at end of last row. Section 1 is complete.

Section 2: Using D as Color 1 and C as Color 2 work 9 rows as for Section 1, joining A at end of last row.

Section 3: Using A as Color 1 and B as Color 2 work 9 rows as for Section 1, joining C at end of last row.

Section 4: Using C as Color 1 and D as Color 2 work 9 rows as for Section 1, joining A at end of last row.

Rep last 4 Sections 3 times more (16 Sections total). Fasten off.

 ## FRINGE

Cut lengths of each shade 14" [35.5 cm] long. Taking 4 strands tog, fold in half and knot into fringe along both ends of Scarf, matching fringe to Scarf. Trim fringe evenly.

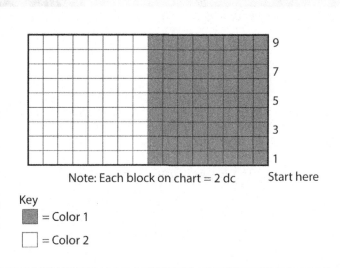

Note: Each block on chart = 2 dc   Start here

Key

■ = Color 1

□ = Color 2

BLISSFUL HEADBAND

This easy-to-crochet headband is made with yarn that looks amazing when doing a flash photo or when car headlights hit it. Yarn has a strand that reflects light as shown in second photo to the right.

TOOLS & MATERIALS

- RED HEART® Reflective™: 1 ball each 8884 Peacock A and 8532 Purple B
- Susan Bates® Crochet Hooks: 9mm [M-13 US] and 6.5mm [K-10.5 US]
- Yarn needle

GAUGE

10 dc = 4" (10 cm) in pattern; 5 rows = 4" (10 cm) with 1 strand of A and B held together. CHECK YOUR GAUGE. Use any size hook to obtain the gauge.

MEASUREMENTS

One size fits mostHeadband measures 4" wide x 22" circumference (10 x 55.9 cm)

PATTERN

 EAR WARMER

With larger hook and 1 strand of A and B held together, ch 12.

Row 1 (right side): Dc in 4th ch from hook and each ch across, turn—10 dc.

Rows 2–26: Ch 3 (counts as dc here and throughout), dc in each dc across, turn.

Joining Row: With wrong sides of Rows 1 and 26 held together and working through both thicknesses, ch 1, sc in each dc—10 sc. Fasten off.

 FINISHING

With right side facing and smaller hook, join 1 strand of B with sc to end of any row on upper edge, working across ends of rows, sc evenly spaced around; join with slip st in first sc. Fasten off. Repeat for lower edge. Weave in ends.

PINEAPPLE KEYHOLE NECK WARMER

Here is a neck warmer scarf that keeps you warm while adding style to to your look. Crochet it in soft, subtly metallic yarn that is a joy to wear.

TOOLS & MATERIALS

- RED HEART® Shimmer®: 1 ball color 1503 Turquoise
- Susan Bates® Crochet Hook: 4.00mm [US G-6].

GAUGE

20 hdc = 4" (10 cm); 12 rows = 4" (10 cm). CHECK YOUR GAUGE. Use any size hook to obtain the gauge given.

MEASUREMENT

Scarf measures 5" (12.7 cm) wide at widest part of pineapple x 34" (86.36 cm) long

PATTERN NOTES

Scarf is worked from center back in two halves. Beginning chains do not count as stitches unless otherwise stated.

SPECIAL STITCHES

Hdc dec (half double crochet decrease) = Yo, [draw up a loop in next st] twice, yo, draw through all 4 loops on hook.

Popcorn = 7 dc in indicated place, remove hook, insert hook in first dc made, draw loop removed from hook through first dc, ch 1 to close.

Fhdc (foundation half double crochet) = Ch 2, yo, pull up a loop in 2nd ch from hook, ch 1 (base ch completed), yo, pull through 3 loops on hook (first hdc completed); for next st: *yo, pull up a loop in last base ch completed, ch 1 (base ch completed), yo, pull through all 3 loops on hook (hdc completed); repeat from * as stated.

PATTERN

 SCARF

First Half

Row 1 (Right Side): 17 fhdc, turn—17 sts.

Note: Work remaining rows in back loops unless otherwise stated.

Rows 2–23: Ch 1, hdc in each st across, turn— 17 sts.

Row 24: Ch 1, hdc in first st, hdc dec in next 2 sts, hdc in each st across to last 3 sts, hdc dec in next 2 sts, hdc in last st, turn—15 sts.

Rows 25–29: Repeat Row 24—5 sts at end of last row.

Row 30: Now working in both lps, ch 3 (counts as dc), (dc, ch 1, 2 dc) in first st, ch 7, skip 3 sts, (2 dc, ch 1, 2 dc) in last st, turn—8 dc, 2 ch-1 spaces, 1 ch-7 space.

Row 31: Ch 2, (2 dc, ch 1, 2 dc) in next ch-1 space, ch 2, skip 3 chs, (dc, ch 1, dc) in next ch, ch 2, skip 3 chs, (2 dc, ch 1, 2 dc) in next ch-1 space, turn—10 dc, 3 ch-1 spaces, 2 ch-2 spaces.

Row 32: Ch 2, (2 dc, ch 1, 2 dc) in next ch-1 space, ch 2, (dc, ch 1, dc) in next ch-1 space, ch 2, (2 dc, ch 1, 2 dc) in next ch-1 space, turn—10 dc, 3 ch-1 spaces, 2 ch-2 spaces.

Row 33: Ch 2, (2 dc, ch 1, 2 dc) in next ch-1 space, ch 3, (2 dc, ch 2, 2 dc) in next ch-1 space, ch 3, (2 dc, ch 1, 2 dc) in next ch-1 space, turn—12 dc, 2 ch-1 spaces, 1 ch-2 space, 2 ch-3 spaces.

Row 34: Ch 2, (2 dc, ch 1, 2 dc) in next ch-1 space, ch 3, 7 dc in ch-2 space, ch 3, (2 dc, ch 1, 2 dc) in next ch-1 space, turn—15 dc, 2 ch-1 spaces, 2 ch-3 spaces.

Row 35: Ch 2, (2 dc, ch 1, 2 dc) in next ch-1 space, ch 2, [dc in next dc, ch 1] 6 times, dc in next dc, ch 2, (2 dc, ch 1, 2 dc) in next ch-1 space, turn—15 dc, 8 ch-1 spaces, 2 ch-2 spaces.

Row 36: Ch 2, (2 dc, ch 1, 2 dc) in next ch-1 space, ch 2, [sc in next ch-1 space, ch 2] 5 times, sc in next ch-1 space, ch 2, (2 dc, ch 1, 2 dc) in next ch-1 space, turn—8 dc, 2 ch-1 spaces, 7 ch-2 spaces, 6 sc.

Row 37: Ch 2, (2 dc, ch 1, 2 dc) in next ch-1 space, ch 2, skip next ch-2 space, [popcorn in next ch-2 space, ch 2, sc in next ch-2 space, ch 2] 2 times, popcorn in next ch-2 space, ch 2, (2 dc, ch 1, 2 dc) in next ch-1 space, turn—8 dc, 2 ch-1 spaces, 6 ch-2 spaces, 3 popcorns.

Row 38: Ch 2, (2 dc, ch 1, 2 dc) in next ch-1 space, ch 3, skip next ch-2 space, [sc in next ch-2 space, ch 3] 4 times, (2 dc, ch 1, 2 dc) in next ch-1 space, turn—8 dc, 2 ch-1 spaces, 5 ch-3 spaces, 4 sc.

Row 39: Ch 2, (2 dc, ch 1, 2 dc) in next ch-1 space, ch 3, skip next ch-3 space, popcorn in next ch-3 space, ch 2, sc in next ch-3 space, ch 2, popcorn in next ch-3 space, ch 3, (2 dc, ch 1, 2 dc) in next ch-1 space, turn—8 dc, 2 ch-1 spaces, 2 ch-2 spaces, 2 popcorns, 1 sc, 2 ch-3 spaces.

Row 40: Ch 2, (2 dc, ch 1, 2 dc) in next ch-1 space, ch 4, sc in next ch-2 space, ch 3, sc in next ch-2 space, ch 4, (2 dc, ch 1, 2 dc) in next ch-1 space, turn—8 dc, 2 ch-1 spaces, 2 ch-4 spaces, 2 sc, 1 ch-3 space.

Row 41: Ch 2, (2 dc, ch 1, 2 dc) in next ch-1 space, ch 4, popcorn in ch-3 space, ch 4, (2 dc, ch 1, 2 dc) in next ch-1 space, turn—8 dc, 2 ch-1 spaces, 2 ch-4 spaces, 1 popcorn.

Row 42: Ch 2, (2 dc, ch 1, 2 dc) in next ch-1 space, ch 3, sc in popcorn, ch 3, (2 dc, ch 1, 2 dc) in next ch-1 space, turn—8 dc, 2 ch-1 spaces, 2 ch-3 spaces, 1 sc.

Row 43: Ch 2, (2 dc, ch 1, 2 dc) in next ch-1 space, (2 dc, ch 1, 2 dc, hdc) in next ch-1 space, turn—8 dc, 2 ch-1 spaces, 1 hdc.

Row 44: Ch 1, slip st in each of next 2 dc, slip st in ch-1 space, ch 5, slip st in next ch-1 space, slip st in each of next 2 dc, fasten off.

Second Half

Row 1: With right side facing and working in opposite side of foundation sts, join with hdc in back loop of first st, hdc in back loop of each st across, turn—17 sts

Rows 2–44: Repeat Rows 2–44 of First Half.

 # EDGING

First Side

With right side facing, join with slip st in end of Row 29 of First Half, sc evenly spaced across neck edge to Rows 29 of Second Half, fasten off.

Second Side

With right side facing, join with slip st in end of Row 29 of Second Half, sc evenly spaced across neck edge to Rows 29 of First Half, fasten off.

 # FINISHING

Weave in ends.

140

Crochet
FOR BEGINNERS

CHILDREN
PROJECTS

CHILD'S EDGED SLIPPERS

These cuffed slippers are worked in the round, then crocheted flat before rejoining to create the slipper shape. The foot length is adjustable and, because the slipper is worked from the toe, it is easy to custom-fit.

TOOLS & MATERIALS

- YARN: Any aran weight yarn would suit this project
- CROCHET HOOK E/4 US (3.5mm) and 7 US (4.5mm) hooks
- NOTIONS 2 stitch markers Yarn needle

GAUGE

Exact gauge is not essential

SIZE

To fit a child, age 2–3 (4–5:6–7) years

PATTERN

With 7 US (4.5mm) hook and yarn A, work 4 ch, join with a ss to form a ring.

ROUND 1: 6 sc into ring, do not join, continue working in a spiral using stitch marker to indicate the last st of each round (remove and replace after last sc of each round). Do not turn, continue to work in a spiral with RS facing.

ROUND 2: Work 2 sc in each sc. (12sts)

ROUND 3: *1 sc in next 2 sts, 2 sc in next st, rep from * to end. (18sts)

 ## MEDIUM & LARGE SIZES ONLY

ROUND 4: *1 sc in next 2 sts, 2 sc in next st, rep from * to end. (24sts)

 ## LARGE SIZE ONLY

ROUND 5: *1 sc in next 3 sts, 2 sc in next st, rep from * to end. (30sts)

 ## ALL SIZES

At the end of round 3 (4:5), continue to work in a spiral without increasing until toe measures 2½ (2¾:3)in/6 (7:8)cm. Turn. Remainder of the sole is worked flat.

 ## ALL SIZES

ROW 1: Ch 1, sc in second ch from hook, sc to last 6 (6:8) sc, turn 12 (18:22) sc.

ROW 2: Dc to end. Continue to work in sc until sole measures 5 (5½:6¼)in/12 (14:16)cm from round 1. Fasten off A.

With RS facing, sew heel seam. Turn slipper right way out and continue with RS facing. With 7 US (4.5mm) hook, rejoin A to center of heel seam, 1 ch (does not count as a st), working in sc, work 1 row evenly around top piece of slipper, working 1 st into each row and each st across front of toe, ss into top of first sc to join.

NEXT ROW: Place markers in center 2 toe stitches. Ch 1 (does not count as st), sc to first marker, turn 1 ch, sc to second marker. Continue working back and forth in sc, leaving the center two stitches unworked. Continue until cuff measures ¾ (1:1¼)in/2 (2.5:3cm). For a longer cuff, work more rows here.

FINAL ROW: Dc to first marker, remove markers, sc2tog, sc to end. Fasten off yarn.

 ## TRIM

With E/4 US (3.5mm) hook and B, join yarn to wrong side of top edge, work 2 rows of sc to finish. Fasten off yarn, weave in all ends. Fold over cuff and sew in place.

143

PLAYTIME BABY ROMPER

Featuring granny motif detail and adjustable straps, this cute crochet romper is perfect for active kids. Created in summery shades this entertaining pattern is worked in the round and created using a granny motif and stripes of half double crochet stitches.

TOOLS & MATERIALS

- Bernat® Softee® Baby Cotton™ (4.2 oz/120 g; 254 yds/232 m)
- Contrast A Feather Gray (52003) 1 ball
- Contrast B Blush (52006) 1 ball
- Bernat® Softee® Cotton™ (4.2 oz/120 g; 254 yds/232 m)
- Contrast C Sandstone (69009) 1 ball
- Contrast D Pool Green (69010) 1 ball
- Size U.S. G/6 (4 mm) crochet hook or size needed to obtain gauge. Yarn needle. Stitch markers.

SIZE

One size to fit chest/waist measurement 12 mos 20" [51 cm]

GAUGE

16 sc and 20 rows = 4" [10 cm]. Motif = Approx 4½ [11.5 cm] square.

144

PATTERN NOTES

• To change color, work to last 2 loops on hook and draw new color through last 2 loops, then proceed in new color.
• Ch 2 at beg of row or rnd does not count as st.
• Ch 3 at beg of rnd counts ad dc.
• Join all rnds with sl st to first st.

PATTERN

 MOTIF

With C, ch 6. Join with sl st to first ch to form ring.

1st rnd: Ch 3. 15 dc in ring. Join. 16 dc.

2nd rnd: Ch 5 (counts as dc and ch-2). *1 dc in next dc. Ch 2. Rep from * around. Join with sl st to 3rd ch of ch-5. Fasten off. 16 dc and 16 ch-2 sps.

3rd rnd: Join D with sl st in any ch-2 sp. Ch 3. (1 dc. Ch 3. 2 dc) in same sp as sl st. *(Ch 2. 1 sc in next ch-2 sp) 3 times. Ch 2.** (2 dc. Ch 3. 2 dc) in next ch-2 sp. Rep from * twice more, then from * to ** once. Join.

4th rnd: Ch 1. 1 sc in each of first 2 sts. *3 sc in corner ch-3 sp. 1 sc in each of next 2 dc. (1 sc in next ch-2 sp. 1 sc in next sc) 3 times. 1 sc in next ch-2 sp.**
1 sc in each of next 2 dc. Rep from * twice more, then from * to ** once. Join. Fasten off.

5th rnd: Join B with sl st to any corner sc (center st of 3-sc grouping). Ch 1. 1 sc in each sc around, working 3 sc in each corner sc. Join. Fasten off.

6th rnd: Join A with sl st to any corner sc (center st of 3-sc grouping). Ch 2. Working in back loops only, 1 hdc in each sc around, working 3 hdc in each corner st. Join. Fasten off, leaving a long tail for seaming.

BODY

Stripe Pat

*(With D, 2 rows. With A, 2 rows) 3 times. Fasten off D. (With C, 2 rows. With A, 2 rows) 3 times. Fasten off C. (With B, 2 rows. With A, 2 rows) 3 times. Fasten off B. These 36 rows form Stripe Pat.

Note: Body section is worked in rnds, turning at end of each rnd to maintain consistent texture with sections that are worked flat.

 # LEG

Proceed in Stripe Pat as follows, taking care to maintain color changes and carry unused color up WS of work:

1st row: (RS). 1 hdc in 3rd ch from hook. 1 hdc in each ch to end of chain. Turn. 38 hdc.

2nd to 4th rows: Ch 2. 1 hdc in each hdc to end of row. Turn.

5th row: Ch 2. 2 hdc in first hdc. 1 hdc in each hdc to last hdc. 2 hdc in last hdc. Turn. 40 hdc. First 5 rows of of Stripe Pat are complete. Keeping count of Stripe Pat, rep 2nd to 5th rows twice more. 44 hdc.

Next 3 rows: Ch 2. 1 hdc in each hdc to end of row. Turn. Fasten off Left Leg. Do not fasten off when making Right Leg.

Join Legs: 1st rnd: (RS). Keeping count of Stripe Pat and beg with Right Leg, ch 2. 2 hdc in first hdc. 1 hdc in each hdc to last hdc. 2 hdc in last hdc. Working into Left Leg, 2 hdc in first hdc. 1 hdc in each hdc to last hdc. 2 hdc in last hdc. 92 hdc. Join. PM for beg of rnd (Center Back). **Turn.**

2nd rnd: Ch 2. 1 hdc in each hdc around. Join. **Turn.**

3rd rnd: Ch 2. 2 hdc in first hdc. 1 hdc in each of next 44 hdc. 2 hdc in each of next 2 hdc (Center Front crotch sts). 1 hdc in each hdc to last hdc. 2 hdc in last hdc. 96 hdc. Join. **Turn.**

Next 31 rnds: Ch 2. 1 hdc in each hdc around. Join. **Turn.**

Fasten off at end of last rnd.

Sew Leg inseams.

Join Motifs to Body: Fold Body flat and mark center front st. Mark 9th st on each side of center st. 19 sts total for Motif. Rep for Back. With RS facing of Motif and Body, place Motif between markers. Whipstitch Motif to Front as shown in photo tutorial. Whipstitch is worked from center hdc of first to last 3-hdc corner on bottom edge. Rep for second Motif and Back.

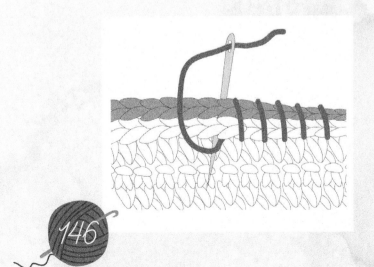

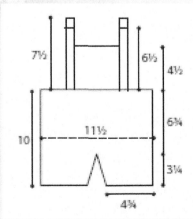

FRONT STRAPS

Left Strap: With RS facing, mark 5th hdc on front of Body at right from Front Motif. Join D with sl st to marked hdc.

**1st row: (RS). Ch 2. 1 hdc in each of first 5 sts. Turn. 5 hdc.

2nd row: Ch 2. 1 hdc in each hdc to end of row. Turn. Rep last row until Strap from beg measures 6½" [16.5 cm], ending on a RS row. Fasten off.**

Right Strap: With RS facing, join D with sl st to first hdc on front of Body at left from Front Motif. Rep from ** to ** as given for Left Strap.

BACK STRAPS

Left Strap: With RS facing, mark 5th hdc on back of Body at right from Back Motif. Join D with sl st to marked hdc.

***1st row: (RS). Ch 2. 1 hdc in each of first 5 sts. Turn. 5 hdc.

2nd row: Ch 2. 1 hdc in each hdc to end of row. Turn. Rep last row until Strap from beg measures 7½" [19 cm], ending on a WS row.

Next row: (RS-buttonhole row). Ch 2. 1 hdc in each of first 2 hdc. Ch 2. Skip next hdc 1 hdc in each of last 2 sts. Turn.

Next row: Ch 2. 1 hdc in each of first 2 hdc. 1 hdc in next ch-2 sp. 1 hdc in each of last 2 hdc. Turn.

Next 3 rows: Ch 2. 1 hdc in each hdc to end of row. Turn. Fasten off at end of last row.***

Right Strap: With RS facing, join D with sl st to first hdc on back of Body at left from Back Motif. Rep from *** to *** as given for Left Strap. Sew Straps into place along Motif edge. Try Romper on. Fold Right Back Strap (with buttonhole) over corresponding Front Strap. PM on Front Strap to correspond to buttonhole for Bobble placement.

With RS facing, join D with sl st at Front Strap marker. Ch 3 (does not count as st). Bobble in same sp as sl st. Sl st in same sp as first sl st. Do not fasten off. Remove loop from crochet hook and place loop around Bobble base, extending loop as needed to fit. Pull yarn end to secure.

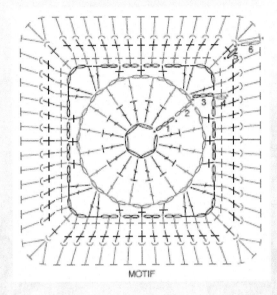

MOTIF

GINGHAM BLANKET

- This toasty crochet blanket features easy double crochet motifs that are joined together to form a classic gingham pattern. Worked in 3 shades of Bernat Baby Blanket, this machine-washable blanket stitches up fast and is a great take-along project. We used soothing blues, but the pattern would be equally cozy in any gentle shades. After motifs are sewn together, a half-double crochet border is applied. Measuring a versatile 37", it's ideal for the nursery or car.

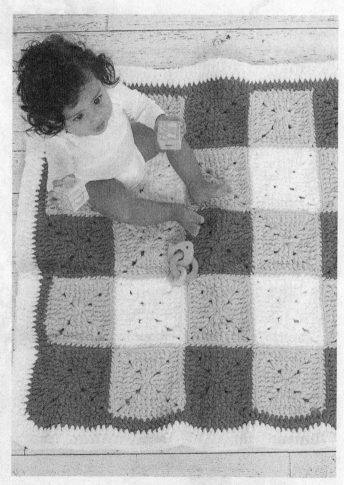

TOOLS & MATERIALS

- Bernat® Baby Blanket™ (10.5 oz/300 g; 220 yds/201 m)
- Contrast A Baby Denim (04115) 1 ball
- Contrast B Baby Blue (04202) 1 ball
- Contrast C Vanilla (04008) 1 ball
- Size U.S. L/11 (8 mm) crochet hook or size needed to obtain gauge.
- Yarn needle.

SIZE

Approx 37" [94 cm] square.

GAUGE

7 sc and 8 rows = 4" [10 cm]. Motif = 7" [18 cm] square.

PATTERN

 MOTIF

Make 9 in A
Make 12 in B
Make 4 in C
Ch 4. Join with sl st to first ch to form ring.

1st rnd: Ch 5 (counts as dc and ch 2). (3 dc in ring. Ch 2) 3 times. 2 dc in ring. Join with sl st to 3rd ch of ch 5.

2nd rnd: Sl st in next ch-2 sp. Ch 5 (counts as dc and ch 2). *2 dc in same sp. 1 dc in each dc to next ch-2 sp. 2 dc in ch-2 sp. Ch 2. Rep from * twice more. 2 dc in same sp. 1 dc in each dc to next ch-2 sp. 1 dc in same sp as ch 5. Join with sl st to 3rd ch of ch 5.

3rd rnd: Sl st in next ch-2 sp. Ch 5 (counts as dc and ch 2). *2 dc in same sp. 1 dc in each dc to next ch-2 sp. 2 dc in ch-2 sp. Ch 2. Rep from * twice more. 2 dc in same sp. 1 dc in each dc to next ch-2 sp. 1 dc in same sp as ch 5. Join with sl st to 3rd ch of ch 5. Fasten off.

 FINISHING

Sew Motifs tog through back loops only as shown in diagram.

Edging: 1st rnd: (RS). Join A with sl st to any corner. Ch 2 (does not count as hdc). Work 1 rnd of hdc evenly around all sides, working 3 hdc in each corner. Join C with sl st to first hdc.

2nd and 3rd rnds: With C, ch 2 (does not count as hdc). 1 hdc in each hdc around, working 3 hdc in each corner hdc. Join with sl st to first hdc. Fasten off at end of 3rd rnd.

A	B	A	B	A
B	C	B	C	B
A	B	A	B	A
B	C	B	C	B
A	B	A	B	A

DAISY PILLOW

Adorn your child's space with this delightful crochet pillow with a cheerful disposition. Just one Bernat Baby Blanket gives you all 3 shades needed to complete your very own daisy. Joined as you work, this whimsical pillow (or toy) is a simple project to crochet and requires minimal finishing. The pattern will keep you engaged with single crochet, simple increases, decreases, and embroidery techniques. It's a forever flower that will be cherished by kids of all ages!

TOOLS & MATERIALS

- Bernat® Baby Blanket™ (10.5 oz/300 g; 220 yds/201 m)
- Contrast A Vanilla (04008) 1 ball
- Contrast B Little Leaf (04796) 1 ball
- Contrast C Buttercup (04746) 1 ball
- Note: 1 ball of Contrast A, B and C will make 3 Pillows.
- Size U.S. K/10½ (6.5 mm) crochet hook or size needed to obtain gauge. Stuffing.
- Stitch marker. Yarn needle. Small amount of Black worsted weight yarn for embroidery.

SIZE

Approx 21" [53.5 cm] diameter.

GAUGE

9 sc and 9 rnds = 4" (10 cm).

PATTERN NOTES

- Do not join at end of rnds.

Work rnds in continuous spiral, placing marker on first st and moving marker each subsequent rnd.

PATTERN

 ## FLOWER CENTER (MAKE 2).

With C, ch 2.

1st rnd: 8 sc in 2nd ch from hook. 8 sc. PM for beg of rnd.

2nd rnd: 2 sc in each sc around. 16 sc.

3rd rnd: *2 sc in next sc. 1 sc in next sc. Rep from * around. 24 sc. Sl st in each of next 2 sc. Fasten off.

 ## FIRST PETAL

With A, ch 16. Join with sl st to form ring, being careful not to twist.

1st rnd: Ch 1. 1 sc in each ch around. 16 sc. PM for beg of rnd.

****2nd rnd:** 1 sc in each sc around.

3rd rnd: *2 sc in next sc. 1 sc in each of next 3 sc. Rep from * around. 20 sc.

4th rnd: 1 sc in each sc around.

5th rnd: *2 sc in next sc. 1 sc in each of next 4 sc. Rep from * around. 24 sc.

6th rnd: 1 sc in each sc around.

7th rnd: *2 sc in next sc. 1 sc in each of next 5 sc. Rep from * around. 28 sc.

8th and 9th rnds: 1 sc in each sc around.

10th rnd: *Sc2tog. 1 sc in each of next 5 sc. Rep from * around. 24 sc.

11th rnd: *Sc2tog. 1 sc in each of next 4 sc. Rep from * around. 20 sc.

12th rnd: *Sc2tog. 1 sc in each of next 3 sc. Rep from * around. 16 sc.

13th rnd: *Sc2tog. 1 sc in next sc. Rep from * around. 12 sc.

14th rnd: *Sc2tog. Rep from * around. 8 sc. Break yarn. Weave end through rem sts and fasten securely. Stuff Petal.**

 ## SECOND PETAL

With B, ch 12.

1st rnd: Working into opposite side of foundation ch of First Petal, 1 sc in each of first 4 ch. Working into beg ch created before first 4 sc, 1 sc in each of first 12 ch. Do not join. 16 sc. PM for beg of rnd. Work in continuous spiral for each subsequent rnd. 16 sc. Work from ** to ** as given for First Petal.

THIRD PETAL

With C, ch 12.

1st rnd: Working into opposite side of foundation ch of previous Petal, skip first 4 ch. 1 sc in each of next 4 ch. Working into beg ch created before first 4 sc, 1 sc in each of first 12 ch. Do not join. 16 sc. PM for beg of rnd. Work in continuous spiral for each subsequent rnd. 16 sc.

Work from ** to ** as given for First Petal.

For Fourth, Fifth, and Sixth Petals, work with A, B, & C, respectively as given for third petal.

PETAL EDGING

Working across opposite side of foundation ch at base of Petal, skip first 8 ch of First Petal (4 ch rem before Second Petal). Join C with sl st in next ch of First Petal.

1st rnd: Ch 1. *Working across opposite side of foundation ch at base of Petal, 1 sc in each of next 4 ch. Rep from * around. 24 sc. Join with sl st to first sc. Do not fasten off.

JOIN FLOWER CENTER

Align last rnd of Flower Center with Petal Edging. Working into back loops only and through both thicknesses, join Petal Edging and Flower Center with sl st in each st around. Join with sl st to first sl st. Stuff Flower Center. Sew rem seam between First and Sixth Petals.

FINISHING

With black worsted weight yarn, embroider eyes with French Knot, and Mouth with Stem St.

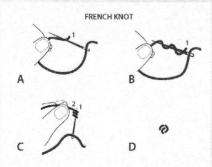

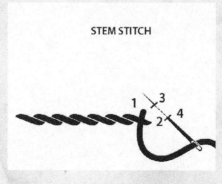

Crochet

FOR BEGINNERS

Book 3

10 EASY AMIGURUMI

154

What is Amigurumi?

Amigurumi is not a word that you con find in Webster's Abridged. Not yet. But with is meteoric rise to popularity, i's only a matter of time before it sneaks its way into every periodicle.

Originally derived from the Japanese, the ward literally means "encompassing knit" in recent years, its come to include crocheted, as well as knitted, plush creations that are defined by one little word: cute. Sometimes overbearingly killer creepy cute, but cute, nonetheless.

Though amigurumi has became the obsession of choice for the crochet community in recent years, the knitting community has been a little slower on the uptake. Even now, if's difficult to find patterns for knitted amigurumi.

RED HEART CROCHET FOX

Featuring our fun Red Heart Amigurumi Textures, you can crochet 2 fantastic little foxes using just one wheel of yarn. Crocheting in rounds, any 4-color wheel gives you all the shades you need to do this pattern. You'll love the textured yarn for the furry parts! Sharpen your skills in single crochet, chain, shaping, increases, decreases, sewing and embroidery on this satisfying project that you'll want to do over and over again!

TOOLS & MATERIALS

- Red Heart® Amigurumi Textures™ (3.5 oz/100 g; 242 yds/221 m)
- Fox (9201) 1 ball makes 2
- Size U.S. B/1 (2.25 mm) crochet hook or size needed to obtain gauge. 1 black safety nose 1/3" [8 mm] and 2 black safety eyes 1/4" [6 mm] for each toy. Fiberfill stuffing. Yarn needle.

SIZE

Approx 4" [10 cm] tall.

GAUGE

22 sc and 24 rows = 4" [10 cm]

PATTERN NOTES

Version 1: Orange as Color 1, Brown as Color 2, White Texture as Color 3.
Version 2: White as Color 1, Brown as Color 2, White Texture as Color 3.

Notes:
- Join all rnds with sl st to first st.
- To change color, work to last 2 loops on hook and draw new color through last 2 loops, then proceed in new color.

PATTERN

 EARS (MAKE 2)

Front Ear: **With Color 1, ch 8.

1st row: (RS). 1 sc in 2nd ch from hook. 1 sc in each ch to end of chain. Turn. 7 sc.

2nd row: Ch 1. Sc2tog. 1 sc in each of next 3 sc. Sc2tog. Turn. 5 sts.

3rd row: Ch 1. 1 sc in each st to end of row. Turn.

4th row: Ch 1. Sc2tog. 1 sc in next sc. Sc2tog. Turn. 3 sts.

5th row: Ch 1. 1 sc in each st to end of row. Turn.

6th row: Ch 1. Sc3tog. Fasten off.**

Back Ear: Rep from ** to ** as given for Front Ear.

Inner Ear: With Color 3, ch 5, leaving a long end for sewing.

1st row: 1 sc in 2nd ch from hook. 1 sc in each ch to end of chain. Turn. 4 sc.

2nd row: Ch 1. (Sc2tog) twice. Turn. 2 sts.

3rd row: Ch 1. 1 sc in each of next 2 sts. Turn.

4th row: Ch 1. Sc2tog. Fasten off. Sew Inner Ear to RS of Front Ear.

With WS of Front and Back Ears tog and working through both thicknesses, join Color 1 with sl st to bottom right corner of Ear.

1st row: With Color 1, work 6 sc evenly up side of Ear. Join Color 2. Do not break Color 1. With Color 2, 4 sc in top corner of Ear. Break Color 2. With Color 1, 6 sc evenly down side of ear. Fasten off, leaving a long end for sewing.

 FUR

Facial Fur
With Color 3, ch 12.

1st row: 1 sc in 2nd ch from hook. 1 sc in each ch to end of chain. Turn. 11 sc.

2nd rnd: Ch 1. Sc2tog. 1 sc in each of next 7 sts. Sc2tog. 9 sts. Fasten off, leaving a long end for sewing.

Chest Fur
With Color 3, ch 8.

1st row: 1 sc in 2nd ch from hook. 1 sc in each ch to end of chain. Turn. 7 sc.

2nd row: Ch 1. Sc2tog. 1 sc in each of next 3 sc. Sc2tog. Turn. 5 sts.

3rd row: Ch 1. 1 sc in each st to end of row. Turn.

14th row: Ch 1. Sc2tog. 1 sc in next sc. Sc2tog. Turn. 3 sts.

5th row: Ch 1. 1 sc in each st to end of row. Fasten off, leaving long end for sewing.

♥ HEAD & BODY

With Color 1, ch 2.

1st rnd: 8 sc in 2nd ch from hook. Join. 8 sc.

2nd rnd: Ch 1. 2 sc in each sc around. Join. 16 sc.

3rd rnd: Ch 1. *1 sc in next sc. 2 sc in next sc. Rep from * around. Join. 24 sc.

4th rnd: Ch 1. *1 sc in each of next 2 sc. 2 sc in next sc. Rep from * around. Join. 32 sc.

5th rnd: Ch 1. 1 sc in each sc around. Join.

6th rnd: Ch 1. *1 sc in each of next 3 sc. 2 sc in next sc. Rep from * around. Join. 40 sc.

8th to 11th rnds: Ch 1. 1 sc in each sc around. Join.

12th rnd: Ch 1. *1 sc in each of next 3 sc. Sc2tog. Rep from * around. Join. 32 sts.

13th rnd: Ch 1. *1 sc in each of next 2 sc. Sc2tog. Rep from * around. Join. 24 sts.

14th rnd: Ch 1. *1 sc in each of next 2 sc. 2 sc in next st. Rep from * around. Join. 32 sc.

15th to 25th rnds: Ch 1. 1 sc in each sc around. Join. Do not fasten off. Sew Facial Fur and Chest Fur to Body and Head as shown in picture. Attach safety eyes and nose as shown in picture. Sew Ears onto Head as shown in picture. Stuff Head and Body firmly.

159

 # LEGS

Left Leg

1st rnd: Cont across Body sts, ch 1. 1 sc in each of first 16 sc. Ch 4. Skip next 16 sc. Join.

2nd rnd: Ch 1. 1 sc in each of first 16 sc. 1 sc in each of next 4 ch. Join. 20 sc. ***

3rd rnd: Ch 1. *1 sc in each of next 2 sc. Sc2tog. Rep from * around. Break Color 1. Join Color 2. 15 sts.

4th rnd: With Color 2, ch 1. *1 sc in next sc. Sc2tog. Rep from * around. Join. 10 sts.

5th rnd: Ch 1. (Sc2tog) 5 times. Join. 5 sts. Fasten off, leaving a long end. Stuff leg firmly. Draw end through rem sts. Pull tightly. Fasten securely.***

Right Leg

Join Color 1 with sl st to last sc of 25th rnd of Body. 1 sc in same sp as sl st. 1 sc into opposite side of each of next 4 ch. 1 sc in each of next 15 sc. Join. 20 sc. Rep from *** to *** as given for Left Leg.

 # ARMS

With Color 2, ch 2.

1st rnd: 8 sc in 2nd ch from hook. Join. 8 sc.

2nd rnd: Ch 1. 1 sc in each sc around. Join with Color 1. Break Color 2.

3rd rnd: With Color 1, ch 1. 1 sc in each sc around. Join. Rep 3rd rnd 4 times more. Fasten off, leaving a long end for sewing. Stuff arms firmly. Sew Arms to Body as shown in picture.

 TAIL

With Color 3, ch 2.

1st rnd: 8 sc in 2nd ch from hook. Join. 8 sc.

2nd rnd: Ch 1. 2 sc in each sc around. Join. 16 sc.

3rd rnd: Ch 1. 1 sc in each sc around. Join. Break Color 3. Join Color 1.

4th rnd: With Color 1, ch 1. *1 sc in next sc. 2 sc in next sc. Rep from * around. Join. 24 sc.

5th to 7th rnds: Ch 1. 1 sc in each sc around. Join.

8th rnd: Ch 1. *1 sc in each of next 2 sc. Sc2tog. Rep from * around. 18 sts.

9th rnd: Ch 1. *1 sc in next sc. Sc2tog. Rep from * around. Join. 12 sts.

10th and 11th rnds: Ch 1. 1 sc in each st around. Fasten off, leaving a long end for sewing. Stuff Tail firmly. Sew Tail to Body as shown in picture.

CRANKY FROG TOY

This crochet frog toy is a great introduction to the art of amigurumi! Stitched in Red Heart Super Saver, simple shaping is used to create a cute, graphic toy. We've given it a grumpy expression for a fun alternative to a stress ball, but you can customize it to create a smiling toy. You'll learn a variety of techniques, including single crochet, working in the round, simple shaping, and more. Measuring approx. 3" tall by 3" wide, it's a "rabbeting" addition to your toy collection!

TOOLS & MATERIALS

- Red Heart® Super Saver™ (7 oz/198 g; 364 yds/333 m)
- Spring Green (0672) 1 ball
- Note: 1 ball of yarn will make 8 toys.
- Size U.S. G/6 [4 mm] crochet hook or size needed to obtain gauge. Yarn needle. Stitch marker. Pair of ¾" [15 mm] safety eyes. Small quantity of black worsted weight yarn or embroidery floss.

SIZE

Approx 3" [7.5 cm] tall by 3" [7.5 cm] in diameter.

GAUGE

14 sc and 15 rows = 4" [10 cm].

162

PATTERN NOTES

Note: Toy is worked in a spiral.
Do not join rnds. There are no ch worked at beg of rnd unless otherwise indicated; simply work directly into the next st (noting marker to indicate end of rnd will move up each rnd).

PATTERN

 ## FROG

Ch 4. Join with sl st to first ch to form ring.

1st rnd: Ch 1. 10 sc in ring. PM on last st.

2nd rnd: *1 sc in next sc. 2 sc in next sc. Rep from * around. 15 sc.

3rd rnd: *1 sc in each of next 2 sc. 2 sc in next sc. Rep from * around. 20 sc.

4th rnd: 1 sc in each sc around.

5th rnd: *1 sc in each of next 3 sc. 2 sc in next sc. Rep from * around. 25 sc.

6th rnd: *1 sc in each of next 4 sc. 2 sc in next sc. Rep from * around. 30 sc.

7th rnd: 1 sc in each sc around.

8th rnd: *1 sc in each of next 5 sc. 2 sc in next sc. Rep from * around. 35 sc.

9th to 13th rnds: 1 sc in each sc around.

14th rnd: 1 scbl in each sc around.

15th rnd: *Working through both loops, 1 sc in each of next 5 sc. Sc2tog. Rep from * around. 30 sts.

16th rnd: *1 sc in each of next 4 sts. Sc2tog. Rep from * around. 25 sts.

17th rnd: *1 sc in each of next 3 sts. Sc2tog. Rep from * around. 20 sts.

Stuff toy. Following manufacturer's instructions, attach safety eyes, placing eyes in approx 8th rnd of work, with 4 sts between eyes. Using back stitch embroider mouth as shown in photo. Work two backstitches directly above Eyes for eyelids.

18th rnd: *1 sc in each of next 2 sts. Sc2tog. Rep from * around. 15 sts.

19th rnd: *1 sc in next st. Sc2tog. Rep from * around. 10 sts.

20th rnd: *Sc2tog. Rep from * around. 5 sts. Fasten off. Draw end tightly through rem sts and secure tightly.

 ## ARMS

Ch 6.

1st row: Sl st in 2nd ch from hook. 1 sl st in each of next 4 ch. (Ch 2. Sl st in 2nd ch from hook. Sl st in side of last sc worked) 3 times. Fasten off. Attach Arms as shown in photo.

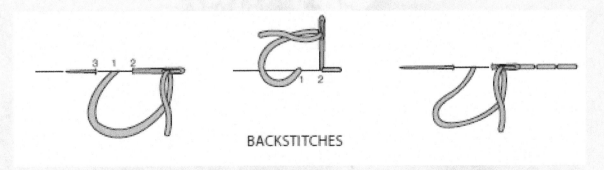

BACKSTITCHES

MOUSE CROCHET TOY

This crochet mouse toy is a great introduction to the art of amigurumi! Stitched in Red Heart Super Saver, simple shaping is used to create a cute graphic toy. We've embroidered a funny expression for a wacky alternative to a stress ball, but you can create any expression you like. The pattern combines a variety of techniques, including single crochet, working in the round, simple shaping, and more. Measuring approx. 3" tall by 3" wide, add this adorable mouse to your toy collection!

TOOLS & MATERIALS

- Red Heart® Super Saver™ (7 oz/198 g; 364 yds/333 m)
- Contrast A Buff (0334) 1 ball
- Contrast B Aran (0313) 1 ball
- Note: 1 ball of A will make 8 toys.
- Size U.S. G/6 [4 mm] crochet hook or size needed to obtain gauge. Yarn needle. Stitch marker. Pair of ¾" [15 mm] safety eyes.

SIZE

Approx 3" [7.5 cm] tall by 3" [7.5 cm] in diameter.

GAUGE

14 sc and 15 rows = 4" [10 cm].

165

PATTERN NOTES

Toy is worked in a spiral. Do not join rnds. There are no ch worked at beg of rnd unless otherwise indicated; simply work directly into the next st (noting marker to indicate end of rnd will move up each rnd). To change color, work to last 2 loops on hook and draw new color through last 2 loops, then proceed in new color.

PATTERN

With A, ch 4. Join with sl st to first ch to form ring.

1st rnd: Ch 1. 10 sc in ring. PM on last st.

2nd rnd: *1 sc in next sc. 2 sc in next sc. Rep from * around. 15 sc.

3rd rnd: *1 sc in each of next 2 sc. 2 sc in next sc. Rep from * around. 20 sc.

4th rnd: 1 sc in each sc around.

5th rnd: *1 sc in each of next 3 sc. 2 sc in next sc. Rep from * around. 25 sc.

6th rnd: *1 sc in each of next 4 sc. 2 sc in next sc. Rep from * around. 30 sc.

7th rnd: 1 sc in each sc around.

8th rnd: *1 sc in each of next 5 sc. 2 sc in next sc. Rep from * around. 35 sc.

9th to 12th rnds: 1 sc in each sc around.

13th rnd: *With A, 1 sc in each of next 16 sc. With B, 1 sc in each of next 3 sc. With A, 1 sc in each sc to end of rnd.

14th rnd: *With A, 1 sc in each of next 15 sc. With B, 1 sc in each of next 5 sc. With A, 1 sc in each sc to end of rnd.

166

15th rnd: As 14th rnd.

116th rnd: *1 sc in each of next 5 sc. Sc2tog. Rep from * around. 30 sts.

17th rnd: *1 sc in each of next 4 sts. Sc2tog. Rep from * around. 25 sts.

18th rnd: *1 sc in each of next 3 sts. Sc2tog. Rep from * around. 20 sts.

Stuff toy. Following manufacturer's instructions, attach safety eyes, placing eyes in approx 9th rnd of work, with 4 sts between eyes. Embroider nose with B in Satin stitch as shown in photo, and embroider whiskers using Straight stitch.

19th rnd: *1 sc in each of next 2 sts. Sc2tog. Rep from * around. 15 sts.

20th rnd: *1 sc in next st. Sc2tog. Rep from * around. 10 sts.

21st rnd: *Sc2tog. Rep from * around. 5 sts.
Fasten off. Draw end tightly through rem sts and secure tightly.

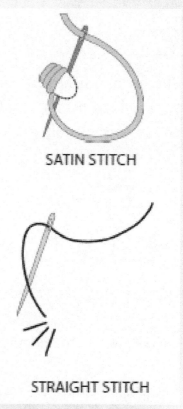

SATIN STITCH

 ARMS

With A, ch 8.

1st row: Sl st in 2nd ch from hook. 1 sl st in each ch to end of chain. Fasten off.

 EARS

With A, ch 3. Join with sl st to first ch to form ring.

1st row: Ch 1. 8 sc in ring. Sl st in ring, Fasten off.
Attach Arms and Ears as shown in photo.

STRAIGHT STITCH

KOALA AMIGURUMI

This cute koala is sure to put smile on your face every time you see it. It is easy to make and is made by simple stitches.

TOOLS & MATERIALS

- Gray and pink cotton yarn
- white acrylic yarn
- Crochet hook 2.5mm (3/0 - 4/0)
- 5mm safety eyes
- Black felt fabric
- Fiberfill for stuffing
- Scissors, glue, needle, pins, a pet brush

SIZE

The size of finished doll is approximately 7 cm (2.8 ") Size of them varies depends on size of yarn and crochet hook. It will still work fine with different size of hook and yarn. Only the the end of finished doll will different slightly.

PATTERN

 HEAD

Gray yarn

Rnd 1 : 6sc in magic ring (6)

Rnd 2 : (inc) repeat 6 times (12)

Rnd 3 : (sc in next st , inc) repeat 6 times (18)

Rnd 4 : (sc in next 2 sts , inc) repeat 6 times (24)

Rnd 5 : (sc in next 3 sts , inc) repeat 6 times (30)

Rnd 6 : (sc in next 5 sts , inc) repeat 5 times (35)

Rnd7 – Rnd 11 : sc in each st around (35)

Rnd 12 : (sc in next 3 sts , dec) repeat 7 times (28)

Rnd 13 : (sc in next 2 sts, dec) repeat 7 times (21)

Rnd 14 : (sc in next st , dec) repeat 7 times (14) , fasten off and stuff.
Insert safety eyes between rnd 8 and rnd 9

 ## BODY

Gray yarn

Rnd 1 : 6sc in magic ring (6)

Rnd 2 : (inc) repeat 6 times (12)

Rnd 3 : (sc in next st , inc) repeat 6 times (18)

Rnd 4 : (sc in next 5 sts , inc) repeat 3 times (21)

Rnd 5 – 10 : sc in each st around (21)

Rnd 11 : (sc in next 2 st, dec) repeat 5 times, sc in next st (16)

Rnd 12 : (sc in next st , dec) repeat 5 times, sc in next st (11), fasten off and leaving tail for sewing then stuff.

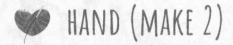 ## HAND (MAKE 2)

Gray yarn

Rnd 1 : 6sc in magic ring (6)

Rnd 2- 6 : sc in each st around (6) fasten off, leave tail and stuff carefully

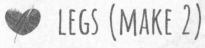 ## LEGS (MAKE 2)

Gray yarn

Rnd 1 : 8sc in magic ring (8)

Rnd 2- 3 : sc in each st around (8) fasten off, leave tail and stuff carefully

 EARS (MAKE 2)

Gray yarn

Rnd 1 : 6sc in magic ring (6)

Rnd 2 : (inc) repeat 6 times (12)

Rnd 3 : (sc in next st , inc) repeat 6 times (18)

Rnd 4 : (sc in next 2 sts , dec) repeat 4 times, sc in next 2 st (14)

Rnd 5 : sc in each st (14) Fasten off, leave tail . (No need stuffing)

 JOINING PARTS

1. With pink cotton yarn, make small line under the eyes
2. Cut felt fabric into a shape like the example
3. Set the head and body with pins then sew them together
4. Pin the hands and sew again

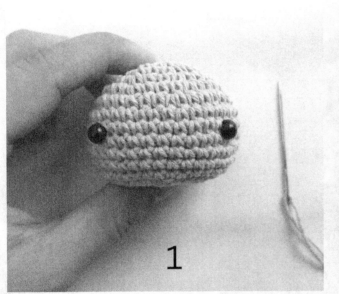

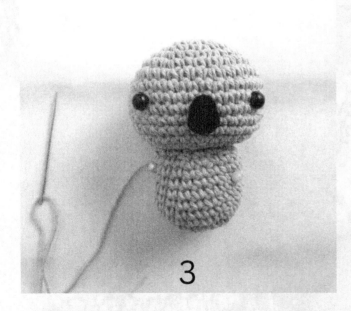

5. Set the ears and sew them

6. Prepare white acrylic yarn for shaggy ears

7. Starting from the lower end of the ear

8. Follow the arrow

9. We will make a knot every 4 ply yarn.

10. Repeat up until the top of ears (6-7 knot)

11. I use dog brush to untangle acrylic yarn. Brush the white yarn slowly

12. Feels like the shaggy hair on ear too long, let's cut out them

13. Finish

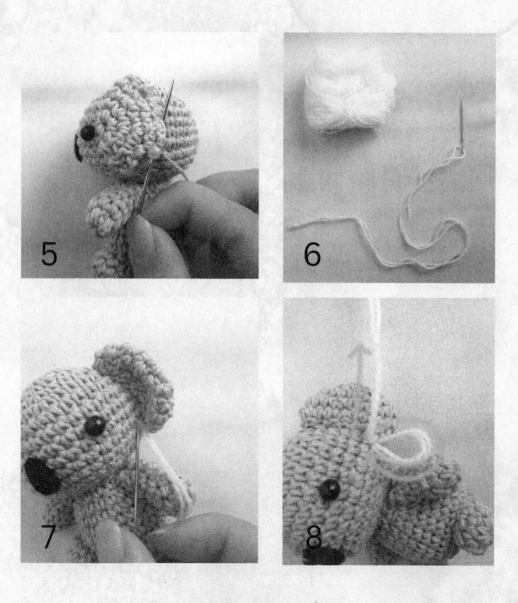

173

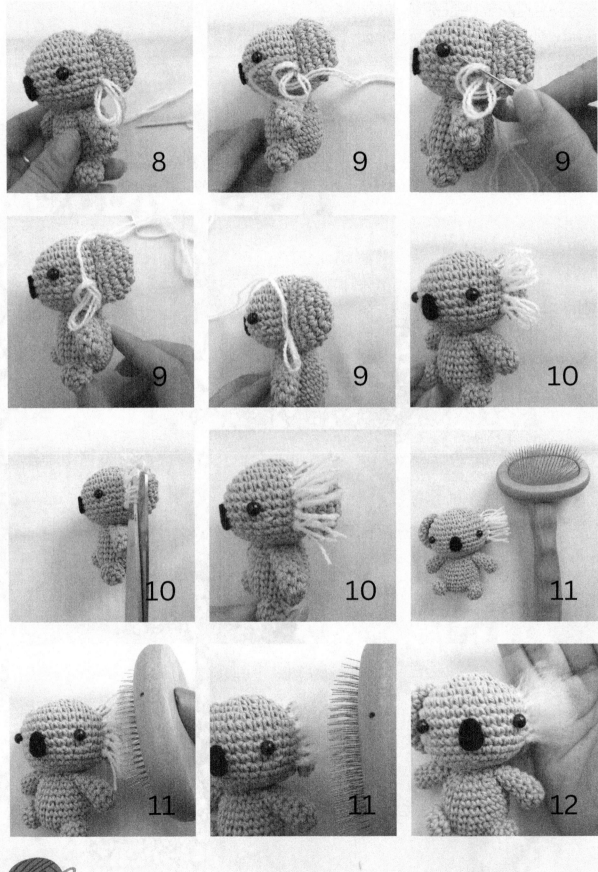

12

12

13

13

175

CARROT AMIGURUMI

This crochet amigurumi carrot is a great project for crochet beginners. It's easy crochet pattern. It can be a nice addition for crochet bunnies or props for photos or vegetables for kids plays. The creative process will definitely brings joy!

TOOLS & MATERIALS

- 1.75 mm crochet hook
- Yarnart Jeans green colour 69, Yarnart Jeans orange colour 70
- Scissors; needle; stitch marker or scrap piece of yarn;
- Polyester fiberfill stuffing.

SIZE

About 9 cm long with semi cotton yarn and a 1.75 mm crochet hook.

TIP

You can use the same pattern to make larger or smaller toys by using finer or bulkier yarn. Alsoyou can use a different color yarn. Pick a crochet hook at least a size smaller than suggested on yarnlabel and crochet tightly enough to achieve a tight gauge that will not allow the stuffing to show through the fabric.

PATTERN

 CARROT

Use orange colour yarn.

To keep track of the beginning of the rounds, use a stitch marker.

Round 1: mr, sc 6 = [6]

Round 2: sc in each st around =[6]

Round 3: (sc 1, inc) x 3 = [9]

Round 4: sc in each st around =[9]

Round 5: (sc 2, inc) x 3 = [12]

Round 6: sc in each st around =[12]

Round 7: (sc 3, inc) x 3 = [15]

Round 8: sc in each st around = [15]

Round 9: (sc 4, inc) x 3 = [18]

Round 10-15(6 rounds): sc in each st around = [18]

Round 16: (sc 1, dec) x 6 = [12] Stuff firmly.

Round 17: dec 6 = [6]

Cut the yarn, hiding the end inside of the piece.

 # LEAF (MAKE 3)

Use green color yarn.

Cs 11, starting from the second chain from the hook sc into next 5 chains , sl st into the sixth chain ,Cs 6, starting from the second chain from the hook sc into next 5 chains , sl st into next 5 chains onthe beginning chain.

Cut the yarn leaving a long yarn tail for sewing and fasten off.

MINI ICE CREAM

Because every day should be Ice Cream Day!

TOOLS & MATERIALS

- 2mm crochet hook;
- Tapestry needle for embroidering the chocolate sprinkles;
- Fiber for filling;
- Mini red pompon (for the cherry);
- Craft glue;
- Yarn (2mm crochet hook compatible) in colors:
- Beige (approximately 6 meters)
- Pink (approximately 6 meters)
- Brown (approximately 1 meter)

SIZE

At the end the Mini Ice Cream will be 7.5 cm

PATTERN

 ## START WITH BEIGE

1- 6 sc into Magic Ring [6]
2- 6 sc [6]
3- (1 sc, 1 inc) x3 [9]
4- 9 sc [9]
5- (2 sc, 1 inc) x3 [12]
6- 12 sc [12]
7- (3 sc, 1 inc) x3 [15]
8- 15 sc [15]
9- (4 sc, 1 inc) x3 [18]
10- 18 sc [18]
11- (5 sc, 1 inc) x3 [21]

 ## CHANGE TO PINK

12- (6 sc, 1 inc) x3 [24]
13- BLO: (7 sc, 1 inc) x3 [27]
14- (8 sc, 1 inc) x3 [30]
15- (3 sc, 1 dec) x6 [24]
16- 24 sc [24]
17- (2 sc, 1 dec) x6 [18]
18- (1 sc, 1 dec) x6 [12]

 ## STUFF

19- 6 dec [6]
20- Inverted Magic Ring
Fasten off.

 ## STUFF

In the loops left over from row 13 (made in BLO) insert the needle again and make: 1 slst, 1 increase of dc*, 1 slst (repeat until end of row and fasten off). *2 dc in the same stitch.
To finish, embroider the chocolate sprinkles, glue the pompon on top and the Little Ice Cream is ready!

TEDDY BEAR

This crochet amigurumi carrot is a great project for crochet beginners. It's easy crochet pattern. It can be a nice addition for crochet bunnies or props for photos or vegetables for kids plays. The creative process will definitely brings joy!

TOOLS & MATERIALS

- Crochet hook: 2.75mm (US size C)
- Sewing needle
- Brown color yarn: approx. 200m (219 yds)
- White color yarn: approx. 28m (31 yds)
- Green color yarn: approx. 42m (46 yds)
- Black color yarn: approx. 2m (2.2 yds)
- Stuffing
- Pattern can be made with sport or worsted weight yarn.

SIZE

The size of bear may vary depending on the size of hook and yarn you use.

PATTERN NOTES

- I worked in continuous rounds. You may use a stitch marker to mark beginning of rounds.
- The number (red color) at the end of each round is the number of stitches you should now have.
- Do not join first and last stitches in round with slip stitch if not stated otherwise.
- When a number is followed by st, that stitch needs to be worked over that number of stitches.

Examples:

- 5sc means 1sc in each of next 5 stitches;
- Sc2tog 2 times means to decrease 2 times over the next 4sc;
- Inc 5 times means increase in each of next 5 stitches.
- When you see brackets, work everything in them as a set.

Example:

- (5sc, sc2tog) 2 times, means repeat everything in the brackets 2 times.
- Each step is separated by a comma.
- I recommend using invisible decrease.

PATTERN

 HEAD

Brown color yarn: ch2

Rnd. 1: 6sc in 2nd ch from hook; 6sts

Rnd. 2: inc 6 times; 12sts

Rnd. 3: (1sc, inc) 6 times; 18sts

Rnd. 4: inc 18 times; 36sts

Rnd. 5-9: sc around; 36sts

Rnd. 10: 8sc, inc 20 times, 8sc; 56sts

Rnd. 11: sc around; 56sts (Pic.1)

Rnd. 12: 12sc, inc, 10sc, inc, 8sc, inc,

10sc, inc, 12sc; 60sts

1

183

Rnd. 13: (9sc, inc) 6 times; 66sts

Rnd. 14-20: sc around; 66sts

Rnd. 21: (sc2tog, 9sc) 6 times; 60sts

Rnd. 22: sc around; 60sts

Rnd. 23: (sc2tog, 8sc) 6 times; 54sts

Rnd. 24: sc around; 54sts

Rnd. 25: (sc2tog, 7sc) 6 times; 48sts

Rnd. 26: sc around; 48sts

Rnd. 27: (sc2tog, 6sc) 6 times; 42sts

Rnd. 28: (sc2tog, 5sc) 6 times; 36sts

Rnd. 29: (sc2tog, 4sc) 6 times; 30sts

Start to stuff the head and keep adding stuffing after every few rounds.

Rnd. 30: (sc2tog, 3sc) 6 times; 24sts

Rnd. 31: (sc2tog, 2sc) 6 times; 18sts

Rnd. 32: (sc2tog, 1sc) 6 times; 12sts

Rnd. 33: sc2tog 6 times; 6sts

Finish, sew the hole shut (Pic.2).

 # BODY

Brown color yarn: ch2

Rnd. 1: 6sc in 2nd ch from hook; 6sts

Rnd. 2: inc 6 times; 12sts

Rnd. 3: (1sc, inc) 6 times; 18sts

Rnd. 4: (2sc, inc) 6 times; 24sts

Rnd. 5: (3sc, inc) 6 times; 30sts

Rnd. 6: (4sc, inc) 6 times; 36sts

Rnd. 7: (5sc, inc) 6 times; 42sts

Rnd. 8: (6sc, inc) 6 times; 48sts

Rnd. 9: (7sc, inc) 6 times; 54sts

Rnd. 10: (8sc, inc) 6 times; 60sts

Rnd. 11-16: sc around; 60sts

Rnd. 17: (sc2tog, 8sc) 6 times; 54sts

Rnd. 18-19: sc around; 54sts

Rnd. 20: (sc2tog, 7sc) 6 times; 48sts

Rnd. 21-23: sc around; 48sts

Rnd. 24: (sc2tog, 6sc) 6 times; 42sts

Rnd. 25-27: sc around; 42sts

Rnd. 28: (sc2tog, 5sc) 6 times; 36sts

Rnd. 29-30: sc around; 36sts

Rnd. 31: (sc2tog, 4sc) 6 times; 30sts

Finish and leave long end to sew head to the body.

Stuff the body (Pic.3).

 ARMS

Brown color yarn: ch2

Rnd. 1: 6sc in 2nd ch from hook; 6sts

Rnd. 2: inc 6 times; 12sts

Rnd. 3: (1sc, inc) 6 times; 18sts

Rnd. 4: (2sc, inc) 6 times; 24sts

Rnd. 5-8: sc around; 24sts

Rnd. 9: sc2tog 6 times, 12sc;

18sts (Pic.4)

Rnd. 10-14: sc around; 18sts

Rnd. 15: (sc2tog, 7sc) 2 times; 16sts

Rnd. 16: sc around; 16sts

Rnd. 17: (sc2tog, 6sc) 2 times; 14sts

Rnd. 18-22: sc around; 14sts

Start to stuff the arm lightly and keep adding stuffing after every few rounds.

Rnd. 23: (sc2tog, 5sc) 2 times; 12sts

Rnd. 24: sc around; 12sts

Rnd. 25: (sc2tog, 4sc) 2 times; 10sts

Rnd. 26-27: sc around; 10sts

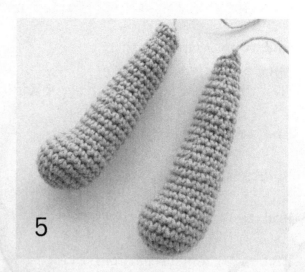

5

Finish and leave long end to sew arms to the body (Pic.5).

 LEGS

Brown color yarn: ch2

Rnd. 1: 6sc in 2nd ch from hook; 6sts

Rnd. 2: inc 6 times; 12sts

Rnd. 3: (1sc, inc) 6 times; 18sts

Rnd. 4: (2sc, inc) 6 times; 24sts

Rnd. 5: (3sc, inc) 6 times; 30sts

Rnd. 6: (4sc, inc) 6 times; 36sts

Rnd. 7-10: sc around; 36sts

6

Rnd. 11: 12sc, sc2tog 6 times, 12sc; 30sts

Rnd. 12: sc around; 30sts (Pic.6)

Rnd. 13: (sc2tog, 3sc) 6 times; 24sts

Rnd. 14: sc2tog, 8sc, sc2tog 2 times, 8sc, sc2tog; 20sts

Rnd. 15-23: sc around; 20sts

Start to stuff the leg lightly and keep adding stuffing after every few rounds.

Rnd. 24: (sc2tog, 8sc) 2 times; 18sts

Rnd. 25: sc around; 18sts

Rnd. 26: (sc2tog, 7sc) 2 times; 16sts

Rnd. 27: (sc2tog, 6sc) 2 times; 14sts

Rnd. 28: (sc2tog, 5sc) 2 times; 12sts

Rnd. 29-30: sc around; 12sts

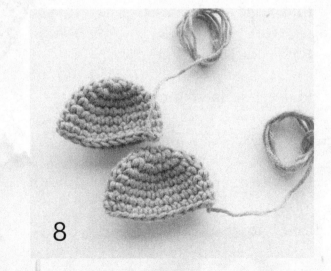

Finish and leave long end to sew legs to the body (Pic.7).

 EARS

Brown color yarn: ch2

Rnd. 1: 6sc in 2nd ch from hook; 6sts

Rnd. 2: inc 6 times; 12sts

Rnd. 3: (1sc, inc) 6 times; 18sts

Rnd. 4: (2sc, inc) 6 times; 24sts

Rnd. 5-8: sc around; 24sts

Finish and leave long end to sew ears onto the head. Do not stuff ears (Pic.8).

 SHORTS

Note: Every round with dc stitches (rounds in green) join with sl st to top of ch3.

First leg:

White color yarn:
Make ch30. Sl st in first chain to form a ring.
Rnd. 1: sc around; 30sts

Green color yarn:
Rnd. 2: ch3, 29dc; 30sts

White color yarn:
Rnd. 3: sc around; 30sts

Green color yarn:
Rnd. 4: ch3, 29dc; 30sts

White color yarn:
Rnd. 5: sc around; 30sts

Finish and end with short tail (first leg only). Do not finish second leg. You will work directly into joining legs and continuing shorts.

Second leg:
Work second leg same as the first leg through Rnd.5. Do not fasten off (Pic.9).

- Now you will join the two legs: Hold two legs together and single crochet one stitch from the first and one stitch from the second leg together; 5sts (Pic.10-11)

Green color yarn:

Rnd. 6: ch3, 24dc (around remaining stitches of first leg), dc inc in st joining legs, 25dc (around second leg) and dc inc in other side of st joining legs; 54sts

See diagram below:

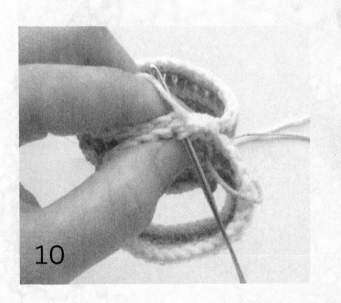

10

11

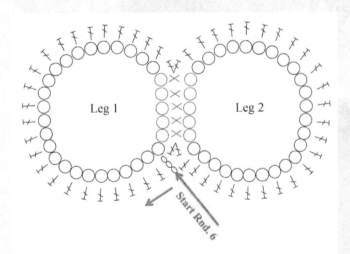

Leg 1   Leg 2

Start Rnd. 6

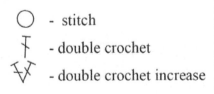

○ - stitch

⊤ - double crochet

Ⅴ̅ - double crochet increase

190

White color yarn:
Rnd. 7: (8sc, inc) 6 times; 60sts

Green color yarn:
Rnd. 8: ch3, 8dc, dc inc, (9dc, dc inc) 5 times; 66sts

White color yarn:
Rnd. 9: sc around; 66sts

Green color yarn:
Rnd. 10: ch3, 65dc; 66sts

White color yarn:
Rnd. 11: sc around; 66sts

Green color yarn:
Rnd. 12: ch3, 65dc; 66sts

White color yarn:
Rnd. 13: (sc2tog, 9sc) 6 times; 60sts

Green color yarn:
Rnd. 14: ch3, 59dc; 60sts

White color yarn:
Rnd. 15: (sc2tog, 8sc) 6 times; 54sts

Green color yarn:
Rnd. 16: ch3, 53dc; 54sts
Rnd. 17: sl st in next 21sts,

Now you'll crochet bib:
- **Row 1**: 12dc, ch3, turn; 12sts
- **Row 2**: 12dc, ch3, turn; 12sts
- **Row 3**: 12dc; 12sts
- Finish and cut green yarn.

White color yarn:
Rnd. 18: sc in each stitch and in the ends of each row 1-3; 66sts
Rnd. 19: sl st in next 3sts,

Now you'll crochet the first strap:
Ch31, 1sc in the 2nd ch from hook, 29sc; 30sts.
Finish and cut the yarn.

Second strap:
Join white yarn in the 6th st to the right of first strap, ch31, 1sc in the 2nd ch from hook, 29sc; 30sts. Finish and cut yarn. Cross straps in across bear's back and sew one to each top corner of the bib of the shorts (Pic.12).

12

FINISHING DETAILS

1. Sew ears to the head. Embroider eyes, nose and mouth areas with black yarn (if you prefer, mark those areas with a textile marker before embroidering).

2. Sew head to the body.

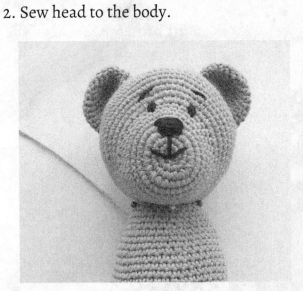

3. Sew arms to the body.

4. Sew legs to the body.

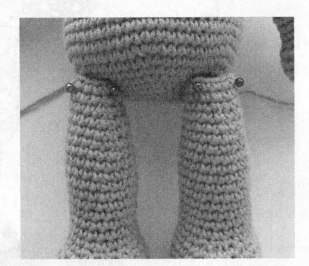

BUMBLE BLOSSOM

Here's a blossom sure to brighten any room or windowsill. This happy flower and her bumblebee friend are the perfect companions for any plant lover - those with green thumbs and those without.

TOOLS & MATERIALS

- 2mm crochet hook
- Sport weight yarn in green, yellow, black, white, brown, and light brown - I used less than a 125m/50g ball of each color when making this project
- Sewing needle
- Stitch marker
- Stuffing material
- Cardboard to stabilize the base of the pot

SIZE

The finished project will measure 12.5cm tall by 10m wide from petal to petal. I used Schachenmayr Catania sport yarn in the following colors.

COLORS

Apfel	00205
Sonne	00208
Schwarz	00110
Marone	00157
Teddy	00161
Weize	00106

PATTERN

 STEM

Using green yarn.

rnd 1 8 MR (8)

rnd 2 -30 8 Sc (8) (29 rounds)

Add stuffing to the stem for added support starting after round 10. Continue to add stuffing as you go.

rnd 31 BLO (1 Sc, 1 INC) x 4 (12)

rnd 32 12 INC (24)

rnd 33 (3 Sc, 1 INC) x 6 (30)

rnd 34 30 Sc (30)

Cut yarn and fasten off invisibly.

Add the sepal to the stem.

Holding the stem with the bottom facing up, insert the hook into last stitch of the remaining loops of round 31 and attach the yarn.

Ch 9, starting in the 2nd chain from the hook Sc 8.

Slst into the next loop in the row.

Repeat in the remaining 11 loops of round 31.

Cut yarn and fasten off invisibly.

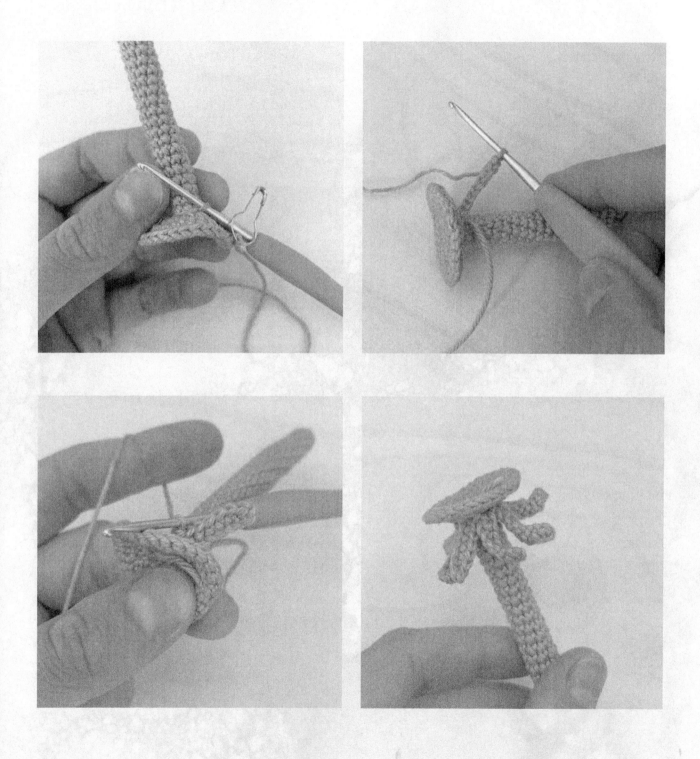

 # FLOWER CENTER

PETAL (MAKE 7)

Using black yarn.

rnd 1: 6 MR (6)

rnd 2: 6 INC (12)

rnd 3: 12 Sc (12)

rnd 4: (1 Sc, 1 INC) x 6 (18)

rnd 5: 18 Sc (18)

rnd 6: (1 Sc, 1 INC, 1 Sc) x 6 (24)

rnd 7: 24 Sc (24)

rnd 8: (3 Sc, 1 INC) x 6 (30)

rnd 9: 30 Sc (30)

Cut yarn and fasten off invisibly.

Using yellow yarn.

rnd 1: 6 MR (6)

rnd 2: 6 INC (12)

rnd 3: (1 Sc, 1 INC) x 6 (18)

rnd 4-7: 18 Sc (18) (4 rounds)

rnd 8: (2 Sc, 1 DEC, 2 Sc) x 3 (15)

rnd 9-12: 15 Sc (15) (4 rounds)

rnd 13: (3 Sc, 1 DEC) x 3 (12)

rnd 14-17: 12 Sc (12) (4 rounds)

rnd 18: (1 Sc, 1 DEC, 1 Sc) x 3 (9)

Cut yarn and fasten off. Leave a long tail for sewing.

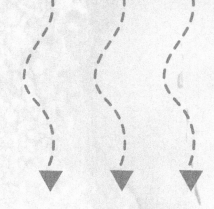

LEAF (MAKE 2)

Using green yarn.

rnd 1: 6 MR (6)

rnd 2: 1 INC, 5 Sc (7)

rnd 3: (1 Sc, 1 INC, 1 Sc) x 2, 1 Sc (9)

rnd 4: (1 Sc, 1 INC, 1 Sc) x 3 (12)

rnd 5: (3 Sc, 1 INC) x 3 (15)

rnd 6: (2 Sc, 1 INC, 2 Sc) x 3 (18)

rnd 7-16: 18 Sc (18) (10 rounds)

rnd 17: (1 Sc, 1 DEC) x 6 (12)

rnd 18: 6 DEC (6)

Cut yarn and fasten off. Leave a long tail for sewing.

POT (MAKE 1)

Using light brown yarn.

rnd 1: 6 MR (6)

rnd 2: 6 INC (12)

rnd 3: (1 Sc, 1 INC) x 6 (18)

rnd 4: (1 Sc, 1 INC, 1 Sc) x 6 (24)

rnd 5: (3 Sc, 1 INC) x 6 (30)

rnd 6: (2 Sc, 1 INC, 2 Sc) x 6 (36)

rnd 7: (5 Sc, 1 INC) x 6 (42)

rnd 8: BLO 42 Sc (42)

rnd 9-11: 42 Sc (42) (3 rounds)

rnd 12: (13 Sc, 1 INC) x 3 (45)

rnd 13-15: 45 Sc (45) (3 rounds)

rnd 16: (7 Sc, 1 INC, 7 Sc) x 3 (48)

rnd 17-19: 48 Sc (48) (3 rounds)

rnd 20: FLO (7 Dc, 1 DcINC) x 6 (54)

rnd 21: 54 Sc (54)

Cut yarn and fasten off invisibly.

DIRT (MAKE 1)

Using brown yarn. The dirt for the pot is created in two parts: the hole in which the flower will be inserted and the top of the dirt.
Begin with the dirt hole.

rnd 1: 6 MR (6)

rnd 2: 6 INC (12)

rnd 3-14: 12 Sc (12) (12 rounds)

Cut yarn and fasten off invisibly.
Begin to crochet the dirt top by holding the hole with the opening facing up. Reattach the yarn and continue crocheting the dirt top.

Tip:
The "wrong side" of the stiches should be on the bottom of the dirt when finished, make sure to insert your hook correctly when reattaching the yarn!

rnd 15: (1 Sc, 1 INC) x 6 (18)

rnd 16: (1 Sc, 1 INC, 1 Sc) x 6 (24)

rnd 17: (3 Sc, 1 INC) x 6 (30)

rnd 18: (2 Sc, 1 INC, 2 Sc) x 6 (36)

rnd 19: (5 Sc, 1 INC) x 6 (42)

rnd 20: (3 Sc, 1 INC, 3 Sc) x 6 (48)

Cut yarn and fasten off. Leave a long tail for sewing.

 # BUMBLEBEE BODY

Starting with black yarn.

rnd 1: 6 MR (6)

rnd 2: 6 INC (12)

rnd 3: 12 Sc (12)

Switch to yellow yarn.

rnd 4 -5: 12 Sc (12) (2 rounds)

Switch to black yarn.

rnd 6-7: 12 Sc (12) (2 rounds)

Switch to yellow yarn.

rnd 8: 6 DEC (6)

Cut yarn and use the yarn end to close the remaining stiches.

 # BUMBLEBEE WINGS

Using white yarn.

Ch 4, starting in the 2nd chain from the hook.

rnd 1: 1 Sc, 1 HDc, 5 Dc in the same stitch, (9) 1 HDc, 1 Sc

Cut yarn and fasten off. Leave a long tail for sewing.

 # FLOWER ASSEMBLY

Begin to assemble the flower by attaching the stem to the center piece. Place the center piece on the stem and sew the pieces together using the yarn tail of the center piece.

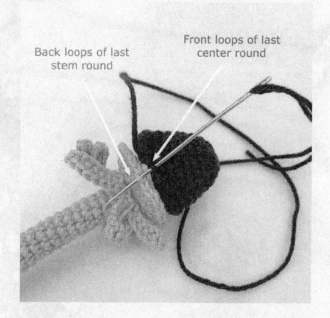

Back loops of last stem round

Front loops of last center round

Add stuffing before sewing the last remaining stitches closed.

another when attached, with very little space between one another.

Attach the petals by sewing along the rounds where the stem and center piece were connected. The petals will fit closely next to one

Tip:
Use pins to help position the petals and leaves before sewing in place.

Attach the leaves to the stem by sewing into place near the 11th round of the stem.

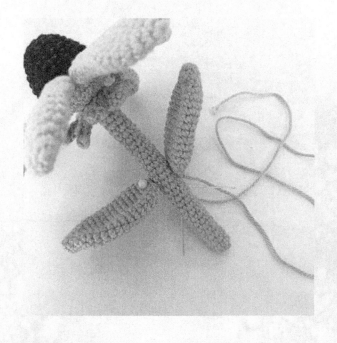

Attach the dirt to the pot by sewing into the remaining loops of round 20 of the pot. Add stuffing before sewing the last remaining loops closed.

 ## POT ASSEMBLY

Add a piece of carboard to the bottom of the pot for extra stability before sewing.

Back loops of rnd 20

Tip:
Take your time adding the stuffing and make sure the dirt hole is centered in the pot. This will help your flower stand up without falling over.

BUMBLEBEE ASSEMBLY

Sew the wings to the body of the bumblebee between rounds 4 and 5.

Congratulations! Your Bumble Blossom is complete!

LITTLE SPARK

Looking for inspiration? Have your amigurumi eureka moment by crocheting this friendly little light bulb. The pattern is suitable for beginners and is perfect for using up left over yarn.

TOOLS & MATERIALS

- Yarn 125m/50g cotton
- Examples use Paintbox cotton & Yarn & Color Must Have
- Yellow approx. 15g
- Silver approx. <10g
- Small amount of black thread for embroidery
- Recommended hook size: 2.5mm
- Safety eyes: 8 mm x 2 – safety eyes are not recommended for young children.
  Alternatively, eyes may be embroidered with black thread.
- Toy stuffing
- Tapestry needle for construction and embroidery
- Stitch marker
- Scissors

SIZE

Approx. 8 cm tall when made using the recommended yarn and hook.

PATTERN NOTES

Work in continuous rounds unless stated otherwise.

PATTERN

Start in Yellow. Work in the round.

1. Sc x 6 in to a MR (6)

2. Inc x 6 (12)

3. (Sc, inc) x 6 (18)

4. (Sc x 2, inc) x 6 (24)

5. (Sc x 3, inc) x 6 (30)

6. Sc x 2, inc, (Sc x 4, inc) x 5, Sc x 2 (36)

7. (Sc x 5, inc) x 6 (42)

8. Sc x 3, inc, (Sc x 6, inc) x 5, Sc x 3 (48)

9-17. Sc x 48 (48) 9 rounds

18. (Sc x 6, dec) x 6 (42)

19. (Sc x 5, dec) x 6 (36)

20. (Sc x 4, dec) x 6 (30)

Insert the safety eyes between round 16-17 with a space of 10 stitches visible between them.

Start to add stuffing and continue to stuff as you go.

21. (Sc x 4, dec) x 5 (25)

22. Sc x 25 (25)

23. (Sc x 3, dec) x 5 (20)

24. Sc x 20 (20)

25. (Sc x 2, dec) x 5 (15)

Change to Silver yarn

26- 30. BLO, Sc x 15 (15) 5 rounds

31. (Sc, dec) x 5 (10)

32. dec x 5 (5)

Break the yarn and pull through. Weave the yarn tail through the FLO of the final round to close. With black thread embroider small eyebrows above the eyes over r 11. Embroider a zig zag between the eyes on r 16. Embroider a line from the base of each eye down towards to screw base of the lightbulb (over r 19-25).

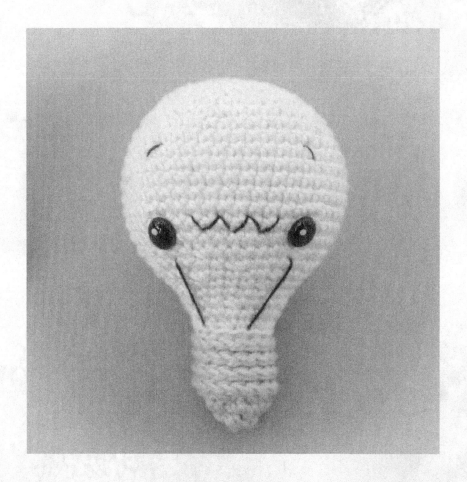

❤ SCREW FITTING

Turn the light bulb upside down, so that the yellow bulb is at the bottom and the grey is at the top.

Join Silver yarn to the first grey open front loop of r 26.

Ss in all open front loops of r 26-30.

Cut the yarn and pull through. Weave in the loose end.

Eureka! Your light bulb is complete!!!

SAMMY THE SNAIL

Do you want your kids to have an amazing snail toy that you made yourself? This project is your best choice. Your kids will love it and you will enjoy making it.

TOOLS & MATERIALS

- 1 x 100g ball of Paintbox Yarns Simply DK in each of
  A – Champagne White,
  B – Stormy Grey and
  C – Candyfloss Pink
- Oddment of black yarn (or embroidery thread) for eyes
- 3.00mm (UK 11 – US C2/D3) crochet hook
- Washable toy filling
- Red crayon (optional – to colour cheeks)

SIZE

Actual measurements
Completed Snail is approx 15 cm/6 in tall

GAUGE

When making a toy such as this, it is not essential to work to the exact tension. If your tension is tight, with more stitches and rows than stated, your toy will be smaller. If your tension is loose, with less stitches and rows than stated, your toy will be larger. However, if your tension is too loose, the toy filling will show through the crochet and spoil the look of the finished item.

PATTERN NOTES

Yarn quantities are based on average requirements and are therefore approximate. Instructions are written using UK terminology with changes for US terminology given in italics in round brackets ( ) afterwards

PATTERN

 SHELL

Make 2 ch using 3.00mm (US C2/D3) crochet hook and B.

round 1: (rs) 6 dc (sc) into 2nd ch from hook, ss to first dc (sc). 6 sts.

round 2: 1 ch (does NOT count as st), 2 dc (sc) into each dc (sc) to end, ss to first dc (sc). 12 sts.

round 3: 1 ch (does NOT count as st), (1 dc (sc) into next dc (sc), 2 dc (sc) into next dc (sc)) 6 times, ss to first dc (sc). 18 sts.

round 4: 1 ch (does NOT count as st), (1 dc (sc) into each of next 2 dc (sc), 2 dc (sc) into next dc (sc)) 6 times, ss to first dc (sc). 24 sts.

round 5: 1 ch (does NOT count as st), (1 dc (sc) into each of next 3 dc (sc), 2 dc (sc) into next dc (sc)) 6 times, ss to first dc (sc). 30 sts.

round 6: 1 ch (does NOT count as st), (1 dc (sc) into each of next 4 dc (sc), 2 dc (sc) into next dc (sc)) 6 times, ss to first dc (sc). 36 sts.

round 7: 1 ch (does NOT count as st), (1 dc (sc) into each of next 5 dc (sc), 2 dc (sc) into next dc (sc)) 6 times, ss to first dc (sc). 42 sts.

round 8: 1 ch (does NOT count as st), (1 dc (sc) into each of next 6 dc (sc), 2 dc (sc) into next dc (sc)) 6 times, ss to first dc (sc). 48 sts.

round 9: 1 ch (does NOT count as st), (1 dc (sc) into each of next 7 dc (sc), 2 dc (sc) into next dc (sc)) 6 times, ss to first dc (sc). 54 sts.

round 10: 1 ch (does NOT count as st), 1 dc (sc) into each dc (sc) to end, ss to first dc (sc).

rounds 11: to 14 As round 10.

Fasten off.

Sew Shell Sections together along top of last round, leaving an opening to insert toy filling. Making sure complete Shell is firmly and evenly filled, insert toy filling and complete seam. Using photograph as a guide and C, embroider (or crochet) a spiral of chain stitch onto each half of Shell.

HEAD & BODY (WORKED FROM HEAD DOWN)

Make 2 ch using 3.00mm (US C2/D3) crochet hook and A.

round 1: (rs) 6 dc (sc) into 2nd ch from hook, ss to first dc (sc). 6 sts.

round 2: 1 ch (does NOT count as st), 2 dc (sc) into each dc (sc) to end, ss to first dc (sc). 12 sts.

round 3: 1 ch (does NOT count as st), (1 dc (sc) into next dc (sc), 2 dc (sc) into next dc (sc)) 6 times, ss to first dc (sc). 18 sts.

round 4: 1 ch (does NOT count as st), (1 dc (sc) into each of next 2 dc (sc), 2 dc (sc) into next dc (sc)) 6 times, ss to first dc (sc). 24 sts.

round 5: 1 ch (does NOT count as st), (1 dc (sc) into each of next 3 dc (sc), 2 dc (sc) into next dc (sc)) 6 times, ss to first dc (sc). 30 sts.

round 6: 1 ch (does NOT count as st), (1 dc (sc) into each of next 4 dc (sc), 2 dc (sc) into next dc (sc)) 6 times, ss to first dc (sc). 36 sts.

round 7: 1 ch (does NOT count as st), (1 dc (sc) into each of next 5 dc (sc), 2 dc (sc) into next dc (sc)) 6 times, ss to first dc (sc). 42 sts.

round 8: 1 ch (does NOT count as st), 1 dc (sc) into each dc (sc) to end, ss to first dc (sc).

rounds 9 to 17: As round 8.

round 18: 1 ch (does NOT count as st), (1 dc (sc) into each of next 5 dc (sc), dc2tog (sc2tog) over next 2 sts) 6 times, ss to first dc (sc). 36 sts.

round 19: 1 ch (does NOT count as st), (1 dc (sc) into each of next 4 dc (sc), dc2tog (sc2tog) over next 2 sts) 6 times, ss to first dc (sc). 30 sts.

round 20: 1 ch (does NOT count as st), (1 dc (sc) into each of next 3 dc (sc), dc2tog (sc2tog) over next 2 sts) 6 times, ss to first dc (sc). 24 sts.

round 21: 1 ch (does NOT count as st), (1 dc (sc) into each of next 2 dc (sc), dc2tog (sc2tog) over next 2 sts) 6 times, ss to first dc (sc). 18 sts.

rounds 22 to 32: As round 8.

Insert toy filling into head section so it is firmly filled, and then into neck section of body. Rest of body will NOT have toy filling inserted so that it can be flattened to sit under Shell.

rounds 33 to 55: As round 8.

round 56: 1 ch (does NOT count as st), (1 dc (sc) into next dc (sc), dc2tog (sc2tog) over next 2 sts) 6 times, ss to first dc (sc). 12 sts.

round 57: As round 8.

round 58: 1 ch (does NOT count as st), (1 dc (sc) into next dc (sc), dc2tog (sc2tog) over next 2 sts) 4 times, ss to first dc (sc). 8 sts.

round 59: As round 8.

round 60: 1 ch (does NOT count as st), (dc2tog (sc2tog) over next 2 sts) 4 times, ss to first dc (sc). 4 sts.

Fasten off.

Run a gathering thread around top of last round worked. Pull up tight (to close the hole) and fasten off securely. Using photograph as a guide, flatten body section and then sew Shell to body, attaching back of head to Shell to hold head in place. Using photograph as a guide, embroider eyes onto head. If desired, use red crayon to colour in circles to form cheeks.

❤ ANTENNAE (MAKE 2)

Make 2 ch using 3.00mm (US C2/D3) crochet hook and A.

round 1: (rs) 6 dc (sc) into 2nd ch from hook, ss to first dc (sc). 6 sts.

round 2: 1 ch (does NOT count as st), 1 dc (sc) into each dc (sc) to end, ss to first dc.

rounds 3 to 6: As round 2.

Fasten off. Insert a little toy filling inside each Antennae. Using photograph as a guide, sew Antennae to top of Head.

DOING BUSINESS WITH CROCHET

CHAPTER BONUS

Doing Business with Crochet

Crochet has been around for centuries and has been used to create a variety of items, from clothing to home décor. With the rise of the maker movement and the popularity of handmade items, crochet has become a hot commodity in the business world. Many entrepreneurs are discovering the potential of crochet as a source of income and are taking advantage of the many opportunities it presents.

If you're looking to start a business with crochet, you're in the right place. This book will provide you with all the information you need to turn your passion for crochet into a profitable business. From creating a business plan to marketing your products, we'll guide you through every step of the process. Whether you're a beginner or an experienced crocheter, this book will help you build a successful business that you can be proud of.

In the pages that follow, you'll find practical advice on everything from sourcing materials to setting prices. You'll learn about the different types of products you can create with crochet and how to create a brand that stands out in a crowded market. We'll also share tips on how to market your products effectively, whether you're selling online or in person. With the right strategies and a lot of hard work, you can turn your love for crochet into a thriving business.

SELLING CROCHET ITEMS ON ETSY

Selling crochet items on Etsy can be a rewarding and profitable venture for those who have a passion for the craft.

Etsy is a popular online marketplace that attracts millions of buyers who are looking for unique, handmade items.

With the right approach, you can leverage the platform's features to grow your business and reach a wider audience.

Let's go through the practical tips and strategies to help you sell your crochet items successfully on Etsy, from setting up your shop to promoting your products and managing your orders.

Follow these tips when selling crocheted items on Etsy.

- Create an attractive shop with a clear and concise description of your products.

- Offer a variety of crochet items in different price ranges to appeal to a wide audience.

- Provide detailed descriptions, high-quality photos, and measurement information for each item.

- Use keywords in your listings to improve your visibility in search results.

- Offer good customer service by responding to inquiries and concerns in a timely manner.

SELLING CROCHET ITEMS ON LOCAL CRAFT FAIR

Craft fairs provide a fantastic opportunity for crocheters to showcase and sell their handmade items to a local community.

Selling crocheted items at a craft fair allows you to connect with potential customers face-to-face and receive valuable feedback on your products.

Let me guide you through the process of preparing for a craft fair, including selecting the right products, pricing, and creating a visually appealing display.

I'll also share tips on how to effectively promote your booth and interact with customers to maximize sales and grow your business.

- Research local craft fairs to find those that are a good fit for your crochet items.

- Prepare a visually appealing display to showcase your crochet items.

- Offer a variety of items in different price ranges to appeal to a wide audience.

- Bring business cards and flyers to hand out to potential customers.

- Offer discounts and promotions to attract customers and increase sales.

216

SELLING CROCHET ITEMS ONLINE

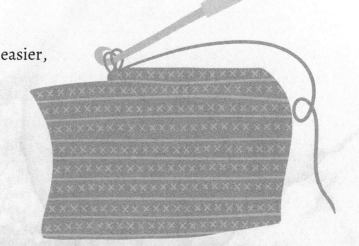

Selling crocheted items online has never been easier, thanks to the wide range of e-commerce platforms available today. With just a few clicks, you can set up an online store and start selling your handmade items to customers around the world. Let us now discuss how you can actually sell your crocheted work online.

- Create an attractive website or online store to sell your crochet items.

- Offer a variety of items in different price ranges to appeal to a wide audience.

- Provide detailed descriptions, high-quality photos, and measurement information for each item.

- Use keywords in your listings to improve your visibility in search results.

- Offer good customer service by responding to inquiries and concerns in a timely manner.

- Use social media and online advertising to promote your store and attract new customers.

- Offer promotions and discounts to attract new customers and retain repeat customers.

- Keep your store and listings up-to-date with new and popular products.

STARTING A YOUTUBE CHANNEL

Starting a YouTube channel for crochet can be a fun and rewarding way to share your passion with a global audience while earning money.

With millions of people interested in learning about crochet, there is a huge potential audience for this type of content.

Let us now discuss how you can start a YouTube channel for crochet and the things to keep in mind.

- Choose a niche for your channel that is related to crochet, such as tutorials, pattern reviews, or product showcases.

- Plan and create high-quality content that is engaging and informative.

- Promote your channel on social media and other relevant websites.

- Interact with your audience by responding to comments and questions.

- Collaborate with other crochet influencers and brands to expand your reach.

- Offer exclusive content and promotions for your followers to incentivize them to subscribe to your channel.

- Continuously improve and evolve your content to keep your audience engaged and growing.

Conclusion

In conclusion, I hope this book has been a valuable resource for you in your journey to learn crochet. Whether you are a complete beginner or someone looking to refresh your skills, I hope you have found the step-by-step instructions and clear illustrations helpful. Crochet is a wonderful hobby that can be both relaxing and fulfilling, and I am delighted to have had the opportunity to share my love of it with you.

Thank you for purchasing the Crochet book. I hope you enjoyed it and found it useful. Writing this book has been a labor of love for me, and I am grateful for the chance to have shared my knowledge and experience with you. I kindly ask you to help me out by sharing this book with as many people as possible. If you enjoyed the book, please leave a review on Amazon so that others can learn about it too. Your feedback would be greatly appreciated.

Remember, crochet is an art that can be enjoyed by anyone, regardless of age or skill level. With practice and patience, you can create beautiful and unique items that you will be proud of. So keep on crocheting, and I wish you all the best on your journey!

Printed in Great Britain
by Amazon

41001265R00123